UNDE_____ E

FROM BREAKDOWN TO BREAKTHROUGH

MIRAV TARKKA

Edited by Rhian Kivits

Re-edited by Heidi De Love

Layout Design by
www.creativekindles.com

WHAT PEOPLE SAY...

"Mirav shares her powerful personal story with raw honesty and bravery. She speaks from her heart and her passion for sharing her experience shines through each chapter. It is a roller coaster, and parts of it may shock and surprise you, but this is what has made Mirav who she is today and driven her passion to help people through her coaching work. By the end of the book you'll feel like you really know who Mirav is. There is nobody quite like her. You'll be inspired to take action in your own life, no matter what."

~ Rhian Kivits,
Relationship Therapist, Holistic Healer, Content Creator

"This book is a beautiful testimony of the Human Spirit. Mirav's life story is heartbreaking on so many levels. A deep dive journey to continuous disappointment, frustration, and sorrow that would crush so many of us. But not Mirav. She came here to face the adversity of life and remind us of the Undefeatable Spirit that we all share. Her incredible Resilience is her conscious choice and a gift to herself, her children and humanity. She is demonstrating how experiencing hardship will change us. The hurt and fear that come with these struggles forever alter our perspectives and our outlook. So resilience isn't about going through life unaffected by hardship. It's not about being unyielding in the face of adversity. It's about integrating those hardships into our lives in a positive and healthy way. If you have the courage to receive Mirav's message, to surrender your dead end "autopilot life" and stand up for your Greatness...You will remember that YOU are in fact - Undefeatable."

~ Jay Rot,
Founder & CEO, BeMore Academy

"A gripping, hard-hitting autobiography by world-renowned Israeli Self-Defence Instructor, Mirav Tarkka. Undeafeatable - tells a story of a young woman's journey from a life of habitual violence, perpetual heartbreak, poverty and low self-esteem, to aligning with her life's purpose as a successful entrepreneur, author and sought-after international Life Coach. Tarkka connects with her readers through her raw, real and relatable recollections of life in Israel and abroad. Her story is one of hope, motivation and self-empowerment. She shows the reader that true strength cannot be acquired through gruelling hours working out in the gym, nor does it come from the defence mechanisms, bravado or the impenetrable walls we build up around us. True strength only comes from allowing ourselves to be totally vulnerable. A great read, from an inspirational young woman."

~ Yolande Herbst,
Pure Conscious Therapy Services

"I have always been fascinated by strong women like me, and always wondered how they became this way. I met Mirav when I learned Krav Maga from her and I was immediately impressed by her skills and life experience. When I found out she was writing a book, I was keen to read it. Mirav's book is everything I wished for and more - inspiring, breathtaking, emotional, insightful, shocking, admirable. Women like her are one of a kind. She truly is a Code Breaking Soul."

~ Nina Menegatto,
Princess Of Seborga

"Undefeatable is an incredibly eye-opening book for women, mothers, entrepreneurs and lightworkers looking to change the world, starting with themselves. Truly inspiring!"

~ Marine L Rot,
Founder, BeMore Academy

"Mirav's story is captivating, inspiring, honest and vulnerable (and I am sure should/will be made into a film!) It is an incredible story of resilience, of never giving up and I took so many lessons from it personally about how to keep on going through the hard times. Mirav is a veritable powerhouse of energy, who walks her talk. Her book will be something I recommend to my clients to remind them that they are stronger than they know. A must read."

~ JoJo Ellis, NLP Trainer,
Peak Mindset Coach, Mentor to Entrepreneurial Women

"It's a compelling and heartwarming story about an intense race between Fear of death and love for life."

~ Marija Simeunovic,
Business Coach

"When I started to read the book, I could not stop. First, Mirav's story is incredible and the way that she managed to solve her situation was amazing. It's really a book that you can't put down! You're literally glued to every page!"

~ Petra Barros,
The Duckies Design Store, Blogger, Entrepreneur

"An inspiring story written with a refreshing honesty and no nonsense attitude. The book to read when you feel that life has thrown too much at you and you want to know how to bounce back."

~ Heidi De Love,
Head Of Operations, Whole Is Well, Monaco

"A captivating story packed with lessons for life. The book is so amazing, not only because of the story, but because of the lessons we can learn from the story. Life itself is a lesson and Mirav was able to learn that lesson and rise above everything. I believe she didn't only create her legacy, but she created a ripple effect that will touch the lives of the ones who will read her book."

~ Mihaela Vlad,
Advertising Strategist

"The authentic, breathtaking, genuinely raw testimony of a warrior lady with a golden heart. A dazzling life-changing journey of tears, stubborn joy of living and being human in its purest form. This book has made me fall in love with myself again."

~ Milica Godevac,
Bookworm

"...it blew my mind. Mirav has such an incredible story and her writing style is super captivating and keeps you on the edge!"

~ Sabine Matharu,
TV & Online Networking Community Leader

"OMG, I could not stop reading! A fascinating journey of self-exploration, with a twist of sexiness. A woman going through an amazing journey of self love, gaining confidence and finding true love. Page turning and never a dull moment."

~ Danielle Meijer,
Executive Administrative Assistant

DEDICATION

To Gaia and Xai, my reasons, my love,
my heart and soul, my life.

May you grow up to be strong, powerful, courageous, decisive
women with purpose and power to lead you, self love to protect
you and my experience to teach you.

Mamma

Table of Contents

Acknowledgments & Gratitude

This book came to life after years of meeting 'human angels' and coaches, guides and friends who have helped me to rise, to keep pushing through, and become stronger and more determined in every step of my journey.

I would like to take this opportunity to show them gratitude and bless them, because they have been a blessing for me. I would like to thank all anonymous angels who came into my life, left unnamed, and went away.

Ilana Kimelman, who saved me from the streets and Miriam Hai, who gave me love, food, shelter and wisdom in the worst times of my life.

Dr. Alex Liban saved me from insanity ☺.

Elaine Collins, who guided me with love and patience, through some brutal moments in my life where I didn't believe in anything any more.

Diego Patron, my Shaman, who taught me, protected me, showed me things beyond my wildest imagination, healed my soul, allowed me to be fearlessly who I really am and guided me towards my undefeatable self.

Patrizia Squillante, who has given me hope, encouragement, support, love and guidance during very desperate and low times.

Rhian Kivits, my 'Wonder Woman', who has become a close friend and encouraged me to be loyal to my truth, as well as giving me spiritual guidance and empowerment. She edited this book, created landing pages, graphics and ideas and, most of all, has been my partner for this beautiful journey.

Parul Agrawal, my Best Seller Campaign Manager, who has been so patient, professional, inspiring, knowledgeable and warm hearted, helping me bring this baby into the world.

Rens Kivits, for designing my beautiful book's cover, pages and the graphics that were needed for this 'baby's' appearance.

My first coach, Dario Perlangeli, for opening my eyes and heart and helping me become reborn and relove myself which was instrumental in my finally living the life I wanted to live.

Jay and Marine Rot, my most recent coaches for helping me understand who I really am, what my soul's purpose is and how can I help others with my story. For believing in me, guiding me and even wiping away my tears. For not cutting me any slack, for not letting me give up. For teaching me, inspiring me, pushing me and setting an amazing personal example.

I would like to thank everyone who took the time and effort to pre-read and review my book: Sabine Matharu, Milica Godevac, JoJo Ellis, Marija Simeunovic, Mihaela Vlad, Nina Menegatto, Petra Barros, Danielle Meijer, Heidi De Love, Yolande Herbst, Marine L.Rot, Jay Rot and Rhian Kivits.

I also thank my Lawyer, Avv. Luca Brazzit, for the legal advice and disclaimers.

Special thanks to my closest friends all around the world, who have supported me through low and high moments, opening their hearts, homes and arms for me. You know who you are.

To my fans, followers, readers and anyone who's out there going through hell, or who's been through it and made it to the other side. You have constantly been in my thoughts while writing this.

My family - thanks to them I have become who I am today.

My biggest debt of gratitude can only be read and received years from now, and it's to the youngest ladies in my life, my greatest teachers, my greatest motivation, my reason for everything - my little daughters Gaia and Xai. Whatever I do, I do for you. I will always do my best to teach you everything I know, protect you from all the dangers I can, and love you with my entire being.

Thank you all, I couldn't have done it without you.

With all my heart, Mirav xxx

Prologue

"From this moment on, you are undefeatable. No matter what happens to you, who tells you what, whatever anyone does to you... it doesn't affect you. Remember that."

I will never forget the look in his eyes when he told me that. It was like he saw my soul, saw how shattered I was, how I was in pieces. He carefully glued the pieces together again and wanted to protect me. He was the only one who wanted to protect me, not even I had the power left in me to do that any longer.

At the time, my marriage was breaking apart. I felt guilt, shame, anger and grief all at once.

My two month old daughter needed me desperately, my fourteen month old toddler wanted me all the time. I had to prepare to move to another country and I had to go through surgery. All alone. And I almost broke.

Breaking means you just stop caring. You feel defeated, you no longer have control over what happens to you.

Life will happen as it wishes and you will stand by and watch. You have no energy - you are drained, you are lost.

When I turned to him I was almost there. I couldn't stop crying. I couldn't understand why this was all happening to me.

I wasn't the perfect wife, but I didn't deserve this - or did I? If it's happening, then I must deserve it.

Here comes the shame, the self blame, self sabotage. I am not worthy...and that point is the most dangerous one in your life.

That's when you're really easy prey to all kinds of predators.

I was smart enough to look for something to pick me up. After all, I had two daughters to take care of. And I found my healer. But the healing only started with him. He made me believe I could - and should - have control over my life again. I'd been through worse, and I could go through this.

I wiped away my tears, took a deep breath, looked in the mirror and told myself that I could do it.

And I've been doing it every single day, day after day, no matter what. I went to the gym every day at the same time. I sang, danced and played with my girls. I meditated, trained my mind and yes, sometimes I faked it, until I made it.

Slowly but surely my power returned and I felt in control of my life again, knowing that I can, and will, do anything, survive anything - it's all in my mind.

In Israel, when life gets difficult, we say 'Shayetet' (תטייש). It's the name of one of the Elite combat troups of our military - hardcore soldiers who can survive the worst conditions.

That was my power word.

I would hug my children, tears running down my face, feeling the pain, the loneliness and the fear of the unknown, repeating 'Shayetet' to myself...My mantra.

'I can do it. I must.' And I did.

The stronger I became, the better my life was. I won't lie to you, many challenges came along. But I insisted. Things got better as I got stronger, and a year later, still alone with two toddlers, I already know with 100% certainty that I can do everything alone.

I rule my Queendom. No one and nothing has broken me, and nothing ever will.

I am **UNDEFEATABLE**.

My Dear Reader,

If you've purchased this book you are or you've been in a place in your life that has made you feel weak, tired, exhausted, empty and defeated. You're looking for ways to make yourself strong again, as quickly as possible. You know you have that power but sometimes you're so fed up, so much 'in it' that you can't see how to get out of it.

Maybe you don't believe you can anymore. Or maybe you just need a push.

I want to open my arms to you, hug you and tell you it will all be okay. You can make it. You will make it. You still have that power, you should never lose hope and never give up on your dreams and goals, no matter how big or small they may be.

I want you to know that I've got you. I am here. You are on my watch, on my team, and I will give you all I have. I will teach you all I have learnt with my blood, sweat and tears, so that you won't have to shed any more of your own tears again.

From now on you are undefeatable.

Mirav

Chapter 01
CODE BREAKING SOUL

"Out of the eater came forth meat, and out of the strong
came forth sweetness"

(Judges, 14:14, Samson's Riddle)

When you look at a baby's face, the word 'undefeatable' doesn't come to mind, does it? Sweet, innocent, a little angel and so on...but 'undefeatable'? And yet, we are born as such. With a 100% confidence, expecting, knowing and believing the world revolves around us.

Demanding our needs and ignoring the opinions, feelings and needs of others. Ignoring fear and danger. Putting our desires at the top of the priority list. Not thinking for a minute that anything, or anyone, can take our power away.

Think about it.

It's later on in life when we start 'accepting' that there is an external world. That there are other people. We start getting criticised, told off, told what to do, given labels and colors and schemes, analysed for our every move.

It is later when we let people take our power. In the name of love, in the name of honor, in the name of whatever they choose as their leading flag. Then once we realise it we either surrender to it or do all we can to claim our power back, to become the raw us again, the undefeatable kind.

Alas, that isn't always easy and many of us give up during the journey. Surrender to society. Surrender to habits. To beliefs. To things we don't really want. We surrender to our comfort zone, forget who we are and why we were born. We give in, give up. Live on 'auto pilot', letting life happen to us, instead of us happening to life.

This is where it stops.

Life is about butterflies, passion, taste, surprise, enthusiasm, determination, conquering, feeling the adrenaline, LIVING! Taking 'it' with both hands and inhaling it like there is no tomorrow, feeling, seeing and taking all it has to offer. And never, ever, giving up.

Well, at least, this is what life is for me. And it has been like that ever since I've remembered myself.

I was born in Israel in 1981. My first memories are mixed with warm sand, the sun kissing our skin, my brother and I running around with bare feet, my favourite yellow dress, big red strawberries, the news always in the background on the radio, handsome soldiers everywhere. I remember running to shelters with gas masks, I remember sirens and alarms for the approaching bombs, I remember feeling no fear as we were so used to it and we were conditioned to see it all as a game.

We used to decorate our gas masks and have a competition about whose was the best. I remember long walks on the beach with my father, I remember being mocked at school for being a 'Goya' (non-Jew) as my father was not Jewish, and looked at strangely in the UN Christmas parties as I was, in fact, 100% Jewish and even as a child Santa Claus just looked like Uncle Skip to me. I remember growing up with all these contradictions and the older I grew, the less I had any idea of where I belonged or who I really was, an identity confusion which forced life to take me through hell's corridors so that I could finally find my true self.

My father was born in Finland in the early 1950s and his childhood was a cold, post-war one. He was forced to work in the snow at only five years old, received very little care from his parents and had to take care of his little brother, Matti, ever since he was a child because his mother died and his father worked away.

To survive, he taught himself to show almost no emotion. There was no room for him to develop his dreams, to explore, to live his life, to reach his goals. The only way to survive the worst was to drink, to forget, and to work on his physical body. And so he did. His one dream in life was to become a pilot but, after losing all his hard earned, saved money in the pilot school bankruptcy, he gave up on ever dreaming again. I guess the heartbreak was too big.

The only trace of that dream was in me, as he wanted to name me 'Mirage', like his favourite battle plane. As 'Merav' is a common Israeli name, meaning 'the most' (but not all), my parents named me Mirav, and I lived up to it - a battle plane, longing to have it all - but feeling like I never did. An unfinished journey. The disappointment of a dream that didn't come true for my parents.

Coming from a history of fighters, hard core merciless warriors who live from the dignity and principles of what honour means to them, I grew up hearing sentences like 'death before dishonour' and 'only the strong survive'. I also grew up with someone who was so caught up in these principles that showing any feeling was considered a weakness.

Like attracts like.

My father met my mother in the town where I was born, Nahariyya, on the border between Lebanon and Israel. My mother was the daughter of a Jewish-Iraqui family, also generations of hard core survivors, kicked out of their own country and forced to walk for weeks in order to bring her and her family members to Israel. A family which honored the men and saw women as distractions, almost slaves. She grew up fulfilling her role as a daughter of that family, raised by people who knew sorrow, paranoia, loss, fear and survived only thanks to their determination.

When my mother met my non-Jewish father, her family disowned her. Again principles, honour, and belief meant much more than love, family or well being. And so my mother and father had nothing and nobody, but each other.

Until I was born. Into all this. All the principles, all the inherited, generations of pain and suffering, all the beliefs and mindsets that didn't serve anyone anymore... And into the warm sun and sand of Israel with the handsome soldiers who gave their lives for their country. Sand, blood, sweat, tears, laughter and crying. I was born into that.

But I am a code breaking soul.

I came into this world to stop the habits, beliefs, mindsets and behaviours that stem from constant survival, paranoia, suffering and fear. I have come and I have suffered so much of all of those - to be able to stand up and say, "This ends here. This stops here. With me."

I raise my daughters differently from how they raised theirs. I worked very hard, and still do, to change my inherited beliefs and tortured mindset. I have been working very hard to change habits, behaviours and fears about work, about money, about relationships, and above all about love.

Love for myself, unconditional love for my girls. Fearless love, sweet love, the love my parents and their parents and the ones before (ok you got it!) never had. I came to change it all. And so life has given me a fair amount of pain to gain wisdom, two daughters to have a purpose, a brilliant mind and an unbreakable will. It (life) then gave me a little push, whispering in my ears "Swim! My child! Swim! Or die!" And I swam. I had to.

Sometimes I almost drowned. Almost. Many times I needed help, and there was always help there for me, teaching me to trust and never lose hope or faith. Life always sent me angels and escape routes.

And today, after 38 years of swimming in seas of challenges, difficulties and obstacles, I have become a freakin' great swimmer ☺

But as a result of me being so different, I never really belonged anywhere (until now).

My parents always saw me as strange. They never ever really got me, moving between being in awe of what I do and being totally unable to comprehend where the heck I came from. It was different, for them, with my brother. He always belonged, no matter what. I was the weirdo, the 'rebel', the black sheep.

My brother and I got along as little children but when we became teenagers we started drifting apart, a growing sensation of coldness emerged between us.

We had no aunts, uncles, grandparents or cousins so having such a small family unit enhanced my feelings of loneliness. The walks on the beach I had with my father were my most precious, family-like, 'belonging' moments until they stopped when I joined the military.

I never belonged at school either. I always had a small number of very unique friends. I wasn't a 'nerd', I wasn't 'cool'. I never smoked (okay, I tried a few times to look cool but I hated it), I wasn't into 'rock', I was way too smart to belong to the bad guys group, and way too cool to belong to the nerds! I was never even able to find a boyfriend at High School. That's how different I was.

I lost my virginity at nineteen to a great guy, my first serious relationship, who was twenty three years old. I loved spending time with adults. I adored reading books, walking with my dad, learning and exploring. I was the first in my class, in the whole city, and one of the first in Israel in my studies. I won numerous competitions and had my poems published in national magazines at ten years old! But that feeling of me longing to belong, to be loved unconditionally and feel truly understood and accepted - that feeling haunted me. And, in time, it made me question my worth. My deservedness to be loved. After all, if your own family doesn't get you, there must be something terribly wrong with you, right?

I remember when I was ten years old my father was sent to Angola for two years. My mother cried all the time and I felt an overwhelming responsibility to take care of her. We had no one and I was the only one she trusted. So, ten year old me started feeling guilty for going to social events and parties. I stayed home instead and helped my mother to clean and to write letters in English to my father, as her English wasn't good enough.

I should never have had to feel such guilt and lack of freedom at just ten years old. I should never have had that sense of responsibility for my mother or sacrificed my own needs and joy for hers. It brought years of guilt for anything good that has happened to me. Years of shaming myself. Years of punishing myself.

My father came back from Angola with a drinking problem. He drank alcohol to avoid drinking polluted, wormy water in Angola and avoid Malaria. It worked, actually. He didn't get Malaria. But he did get an addiction. It was an addiction both my parents kept denying. I heard them arguing, and fighting 'in silence' - I saw her creeping around the house hiding alcohol and money to prevent him from drinking and then I would see him creeping around to find it. I had to lie to her to cover his ass and to lie to him to cover for her. I wanted peace in my home, so I lied. But, as always, life bites you in the bum when you do stuff like that.

One day I came back from school and saw ambulances parked beneath our building. I remember wishing they'd come for the neighbour because I was convinced he had poisoned his dog. When I made it upstairs, I discovered the door was open. Medics were leaning over my father, doing something to him. My mother cowered in a corner, white, panic stricken. No one even noticed me, until one of the medics turned around. He took me outside.

"Your father has had liver failure. Your mother found him on the floor and called us. Don't worry, everything will be okay."

I don't remember what happened next. Or later. I just remember my parents never, ever talking about it. Still denying there was a problem. My father stopped drinking for a while, my mother stopped talking about it for a while. And I? I stopped believing 100% of anything they say. I started doubting my parents, I started understanding they're not always right, or correct, or the know-it-all-mighty.

I understood that there is much more truth in life than what I was told. It is not 'only the strong survive', 'death before dishonor' or anything like that. My father wasn't the strongest. My mother wasn't a truth teller or seeker. And I was worthy of the truth and deserved to be honored and respected for who I was - their daughter - not for what I did, if I obeyed, or agreed with their opinion.

Tiny tears in my trust and unconditional love for my parents started to occur but, not knowing better, instead of feeling angry at them or claiming my worth, I started to feel less and less worthy of their love. Of their trust. And, of course, of my own.

A couple of years later those feelings became symptoms and the symptoms became a sickness. I started going down the road of self-sabotage and self-hate. I had Bulimia, and various eating disorders and I would exercise for eight hours a day in my room with the mattress laid on the floor to block the noise from reaching my parents and Jane Fonda's exercise video on replay twelve times in a row.

I plucked my eyebrows until they were almost gone and tore out my hair. I was isolated - no one really knew a thing about me. At school my grades were high and I was a perfect student, a perfect girl who just buried her head in books and gyms. But inside I was constantly criticising myself and I hated what I saw in the mirror. I hated what I felt inside. I could constantly taste vomit in my mouth and I often wondered why nobody noticed.

I swapped sizes like an accordion. I would lose and gain even up to 7kg a week. And no one asked what I was doing in the bathroom for so long, why my knuckles were so scratched and my teeth were yellow. Nobody asked why I wasn't going out with friends my own age or why I needed so many showers every day. No one thought to ask me if I needed help.

I remember one time my mother said that I was gaining too much weight and I should watch what I eat. I told her that her saying that was just like shoving my head in the toilet bowl. She didn't get the hint.

While my brother was always too thin and was encouraged to eat chocolate, cakes and ice cream, I was told off every time I touched it and food was hidden from me. It became worse and worse until I was vomiting nine times a day.

Years later, my Therapist told me I was vomiting my family out of me. I never hated them. I just couldn't believe how little they knew me, how they pretended to know me and how much I longed with all my being for them to actually want to know me for who I am.

I kept on vomiting like this for five years until one day I vomited blood. I was so scared. I had no one to turn to. I couldn't trust any doctor in the little town I grew up in to not tell my parents - something that would not end up in help for me - much needed help - but would result in days and weeks of criticism, making me feel even more guilt and shame and out of control, watching after every bite I have and robbing me of every ounce of privacy I might have.

And so for the first time in my life, I used my brilliance and ability to study - to save my life. I went to the local library, I compiled a collection of medical books, biographies, pictures, all I could find about Bulimia, and I read and read and read.

The solution, ironically enough, was not in the books. On the contrary. The books doomed me to death; they all said that without psychiatric help most 'victims' die or, in the best case scenario, keep on living with the disease. So I decided it was up to me. I told myself that I was strong enough to do this and I promised I would never, ever vomit again intentionally, no matter what. Even if I gained 10kg.

I forced myself to imagine the worst case scenario if I chose not to vomit. I would get fat. I would be ridiculed. I'd never have a boyfriend. And I told myself that it was all okay.

I never vomited again (except for my early pregnancy morning sickness or when I got drunk). I gradually started treating my relationship with food, exercise and my body with more love and care. During the years that passed, I managed to create a whole new healthy relationship with food and exercise. My body isn't perfect and I love and accept it. I work at doing my best for my body without the self hatred.

But the scar inside has never healed.

The feeling that my family didn't know me, didn't 'see' me, didn't care about what I was going through. The food hidden from me, the mistrust, the difference between me and my brother, has deepened the tear that started years before, a tear that would start seven years of war between me and them, a war from which none of us would ever recover from fully.

This was the war which made me a warrior. And it was this war that made me the best mother I could ever be.

Chapter 02
BETRAYAL

"The fathers have eaten a sour grape, and the children's
teeth are set on edge"

(Jeremia 31:29)

I was seventeen years old. Six months before I had to start military service. High school was almost over. I'd done so well with my exams I didn't even have to attend school any longer. But I needed to fill my time with something, something I felt passionate about. What would that be? The only things I liked were weight lifting and reading books.

I remember that morning clearly.

I got up and I said to myself, "I should start learning something new. I have six months to invest in it. Maybe belly-dancing or Thai Boxing..."

I had no idea why those two options flew into my mind.

And so I went to my gym, a few hours later. As I got there, something extremely weird happened. A short, bold, bulky guy was gluing a flyer to the door. As he turned around he gave me a sharp look. His icy eyes penetrated mine. I felt strange shivers, and turned to look at the flyer.

'Thai Boxing, starting tomorrow, 7pm.'

I couldn't believe it. I'd just thought about Thai Boxing a few hours before. I turned back to the icy-eyed man.

"Are you the teacher?" I asked.

"Yes, Kobi." he replied.

I asked if I could join and what should I bring. He gave me the details and walked away. That moment, although I didn't know it then, my life changed forever. The shivers should have told me something. They wouldn't go away for a very long time...

After my training I skipped home happily and told my parents with excitement that I wanted to start Muay Thai. They agreed and I waited anxiously for the next day.

I was at the gym at 18:45, my heart pounding. I wore my shortest shorts and a top tank top (little did I know that part of the Muay Thai warm up would be to lift my leg above someone's shoulder…) I walked into the gym, and there he was. The icey guy. The shivers started in my body again and my heart was pounding so hard that I was sure everyone could see it.

That smell - the Thai oil, testosterone and sweat - they were all men. Sweaty, hairy, heavily breathing, wearing these colourful Thai shorts and boxing gloves.

I was still a virgin and I could feel heat running through my body. I had never seen so many men like this. The adrenaline of the fight was in the air. That was viagra to my body! I fell deeply, madly, instantly in love. With the smell. With the men. With Muay Thai. With Kobi.

Kobi was the first, and the most intense, destructive, crazy love of my life. It was because of that love story that my life contained so much chaos and suffering for the next seven years. This is also exactly how I become a 'badass'.

I remember before I started going out with Kobi, I met a friend of his. We were chatting and he told me I was irresistible to many men. At the time I didn't think he was flirting with me and I had no idea what the heck he was talking about. I was a simple seventeen year old and had no idea about anything in life.

I wasn't exceptionally good looking, sexy or sassy. Not to mention my confidence and self awareness were pretty much floor level.

So I asked him, "Why would you say so?"

His answer has remained with me until this day as it was the last time anyone ever told me something like that.

"Your innocence. It is clear in your eyes. There are not many women like you in today's world. Don't ever lose it."

But Kobi made me lose it. He turned my world upside down. He showed me the best and the worst a relationship could be. I lost everything for him, and eventually I discovered who I was because of him. But let's get back to my very first true love - Muay Thai.

I was the only girl in the Muay Thai club. I joined that club as a complete 'sissy'. I discovered power, resilience and badassery I had no idea that I had. The men in that class all admired the one seventeen year old girl who had so many 'balls' she could go against five of them at a time. Balls, or anger buried inside? Very likely a bit of both.

I loved everything about Muay Thai. I dreaded the coming military service as it would take me away from training. I tried desperately to swap my forthcoming courses for the military so I could just become a normal military secretary and be home every day, which is what most women usually do in the IDF anyway. But the IDF had scheduled me to become an Operational Sergeant, which was part of a combat unit, and I was going to hardly see home during those two years of service.

Muay Thai had me hooked. I used Thai oil instead of body lotion. I was so proud of my blues and purples, I would flash them everywhere. I learned to love that pain. Nothing would stop me from training. NOTHING.

I even got once my rib cracked; I secretly went to a Doctor and begged him not to tell my parents so that they wouldn't pull me out of the training. He checked my ribs and told me that one was cracked. I couldn't do anything about it but I definitely couldn't stop training. Every time I yawned, or even sneezed, I had an extreme, stabbing pain. And I had to hide it away when it happened near my parents. But, like I said, nothing could stop me.

Kobi was thirty three years old at the time. He was my trainer and a very well known Commander in the Operational Police unit of Israel. He was one of the founders of Muay Thai in Israel and trained champions. I dreamt of him, fantasised about him, admired him. Never in my wildest dreams did I think that he might like me too.

One day he told me that he saw I had incredible potential and said he'd like to train me personally so that I could reach a higher level. We started running on the beach together regularly until one day he asked me out. I couldn't believe my ears!

But being the good girl I was, I skipped home with excitement to tell my parents that the man I'd been worshipping for the last few months wanted to date me.

I told my father first and he seemed proud.

"That's my girl!" he said. Great.

My mother was next, but when I went to talk to her, to my great surprise, she went completely bananas.

"WHAT? That old guy wants to go out with you? Over my dead body! You are living under my roof, you obey my rules!" she screamed.

I never understood her.

On one hand, she was always the 'cool mom'. She wore young girls' clothes, she talked freely about sex, she seemed to be my best friend and I would tell her everything. But on the other hand, she seemed very stuck in old beliefs. Me having a boyfriend always freaked her out, me having sex meant I was a complete slut and should be ashamed of myself.

In her eyes I should never spend money on doing something nice for myself, I should never dare to shave my legs or even wear perfume. I had to help her clean the house thoroughly every Thursday, unable to go out with friends or enjoy my youth, while the men in the house - my father and brother - were forbidden from lifting a finger.

I never knew what was right or wrong, I felt guilty each time I tried to spend some time with a friend or in the gym on Thursdays, I was told off all the time whatever I chose to do. I was made to feel guilty.

My mother was Jewish, and my father wasn't, so in our house nothing was clear. What am I? Jewish? Christian? Nothing? Is there even a God? Am I a good girl? Am I worthy?

It was all so confusing for me. This confusion led to a huge lack of identity for most of my life.

My father a big strong man and we had such a beautiful bond, walking together for many hours on the beach. I shared the most important moments of my life with him. And he said I was his little princess. He promised he would always protect me. He was my hero.

I don't know why my mother's voice always won. He never once stood up to her, not even to defend me. And that day, when her screams shut down my love story, he silently joined her.

I was not even eighteen. I was about to start military service. I was scared. I was heartbroken. And I had to make an important choice.

So I decided to obey my mother and forget about Kobi. For now. I was forbidden from going to Muay Thai. My heart was in pieces. The greatest love of my life was taken away from me. Muay Thai was in my blood and I loved it more than life itself at the time. And I was giving up the chance to start a relationship with the only man who made my knees go weak. But I surrendered. I was devastated. A few weeks later, I started military service.

At first, I hated it. It was too difficult for me to be away from my mother, too strange to be all alone. But in time I started exploring my freedom. I started going out more. I made some friends in the base and we used to sneak out together. I took bus trips to the other side of Israel and partied for nights on end.

For the first time in my life I didn't have to obey any house rules. There were military rules, but they were so easy for me to follow or 'work around'. You need to be at a certain time in a certain place, dressed in uniform and doing your job. Salute your Commander and your flag, obey protocols, try to stay alive. That was all. As long as I did that I was able to explore the other side of my life. And so I did.

I went out with many soldiers in the two years I served. I partied, I did my crazy, I got in trouble and I had fun too. I received a bonus for my service. I was able to go to the Wingate Instiitute and learn how to teach soldiers Krav Maga, Israeli contact combat, the most lethal self defense system in the world.

I was thrilled! There I was, in the world's only and most important Krav Maga military training institute, and all day long we would do the one thing that I loved - we would beat each other up ☺ kidding!

It reminded me of my beloved Muay Thai. It was aggressive, violent, passionate and full of life. And it had no rules, like my love for Kobi, which, even with all the men I had around in my life, I couldn't get out of my mind.

During my training we did a 10km run at 5am, then we would train for the whole day, with lunch and dinner break. We had guarding, toilet cleaning and kitchen shifts in between. We got 'three Matkal hours of sleep', which means in the military - the bare minimum.

I managed to get into the base's staff gym and I spent one out of those three hours there, training. It was one of the best times of my life. I learned how to teach, I learned how to use my handgun and rifle as a weapon and a shield, I learned how to kill a man in a second. I could run up a 90 degree sandy mountain with an 'injured soldier' on my back, defending us both from knife, gun and stick attacks, then down the mountain, three times, a Commander screaming at us, throwing 'bombs' at us, and also asking us things in a secret army language. I LOVED IT!

When I got back to my home base, I taught everyone I could, I even secretly wished for a chance to practice my new skills. Military service ended but my heart was still devoted to Krav Maga. I decided I want to keep on practicing it in the outside world and so I needed to get my military diploma converted to a civil one.

The responsible person for that in my area was the one and only Kobi.

We met secretly to organise my diploma. We both knew it was just an excuse. Two years after not seeing each other, when we finally met I could literally feel my heart explode. He didn't wait to lean down and kiss me. He tasted like mint. He tasted like his eyes - cold, icy and fascinating.

I was twenty years old then. I'd completed a full IDF service, which was not easy. I'd held and shot rifles and guns. I'd been underground, hearing soldiers crying for their missing legs, screaming for their mothers. I'd seen blood, war, tears. I'd been part of fighting for something so much bigger than my own personal life; my country and its values.

I'd trained elite combat soldiers to fight for their lives and defend themselves. I'd nearly been kidnapped yet managed to escape on time. I'd been part of secret, nation saving missions about which I'd been sworn to secrecy. I ate the shitty food for two years, lost 8kg and gained almost 20kg, lived in the same clothes without a shower for over a month. I slept in tents, on the ground, in the cold and in the desert. I'd been to Wingate. I survived moments I didn't believe I would.

I'd been with other men and I'd tasted life like never before.

I was ready. I was a grown woman. Now, no one could tell me what to do.

So I kissed him back.

We started going out, but we kept it a secret. He'd just separated from his wife and didn't want to hurt her feelings and I didn't want to tell my parents anything until I knew it was serious. My father was in danger of losing his job, my brother was just about to start his military service, and my house was full of tension and stress. So I really didn't want to make it worse by telling them that I'd started dating him again, not knowing where it was leading. But Kobi literally swept me off my feet. I was twenty, he was thirty five, and he was so much better than all the 'kids' I'd dated all these years. He took me to places I'd never seen before. He had his own car and house. He was my maestro, and became my master.

My heart would skip a beat every time he called and every time I even thought of him. He was my God. And I not only fell blindly in love with him, but I also let my guard down. That is why I, the IDF trained Sergeant, didn't notice when one day my mother followed me and found out about my love story.

I came back home into an interrogation.

"Where were you?" she asked.

"I was out with a friend." I replied.

"Who was it?" she continued.

I responded it was some guy from my base she didn't know.

She started screaming that I was lying to her. I was out with 'the old man', with Kobi. So I confessed. Yes, I was out with him. I didn't want to say anything before I figured out where this was leading, as I knew she disliked him.

She said "I will never accept this man in my house!"

I said, "That's fine and I respect that. I won't bring him here, don't worry. "

But that didn't settle her.

"You can't go out with him." she said.

"Excuse me?? I just completed two years in the military, where my commanders wouldn't tell me who I could see, and you will? I am a grown woman. I waited for two years! I won't bring him here, but I must explore how I feel."

"Not under my roof!" she screamed. "Over my dead body!"

Things were getting out of hand. I looked for my father.

There he was, sitting quietly, looking away, not daring to look at any of us. My brother wasn't home. She screamed and ordered me to make a decision, a choice, right then and there. I either give up seeing Kobi again, or I am not their daughter any longer. I'd be out.

"How can you say this to me, after all you have been through?" I tried asking.

Twenty two years earlier, my mother's parents gave her the same ultimatum when she met my father. They ordered her to stop seeing him or else they'd disown her. When she refused to leave him, they even tried to kill him with a broken bottle. My mother never saw her family again. My brother and I never met or spoke to them. She knew what an ultimatum does. She knew loss, she knew what it meant to pay the price for love. But she was now doing it to me.

"In a choice between my heart, or staying and obeying the rules, I will choose what you chose, Mom. I choose my heart. I need to feel this. I need to find out where this leads. If I am not important to you as a daughter; if you can't keep me in your life and respect my choices, it is your decision!"

She was furious. She didn't see the fact that she was forcing me to give up what I wanted, again. She didn't remember the fact that, until now, I always chose her.

I gave up relationships, I gave up my social life. I gave up parts of my childhood, I gave up freedom. I obeyed the rules and I was a good girl, the best, and I spent every freakin' Thursday cleaning the house like a maniac.

But this time I was not willing to give up. Not on this one. I must feel this. I can't lose again, like I lost my Muay Thai and gave up Kobi two years earlier.

I went upstairs to my room.

My mother followed me screaming, "Slut! It's me or him!"

I was shocked. I took a small bag and packed my toothbrush and a set of clothes. I reached for my allowance money but she snatched it away from me.

"Thief! You don't take anything from my house!"

I went to the door. I looked for my father.

He was sitting there, his head buried between his hands. Looking into space. Saying nothing. NOTHING. Not one word to my mother for throwing his daughter out of the house. Not one word to try to stop this, to protect me.

Coward.

I opened the door and stepped outside. By now my mother's screaming had become a robotic wailing. She was monologing how right she was, how stupid I am and how evil Kobi is. How this was her house, her rules and so on...

I walked towards the road, my body shaking with shock and tears, my hand reaching for my phone. I had no idea what to do, where to go.

"Mirav!" My father's soft voice was behind me.

"Finally," I thought. "He is finally here to save me, To protect me. Like he always said he would, in our endless walks on the beach. I'm his little princess, right?"

He handed me some cash, a few dollar notes.

"Take that, it is all I have. Now go." He hugged me and kissed my forehead.

I hesitated, looked at him, waited for more, but there was nothing.

With a broken heart, I walked away, swallowing the gulp in my throat, knowing I wasn't important enough for anyone in my house. Knowing that all the walks, the words, the trust I'd placed in my father to always have my back and look out for me, was a lie.

He never once looked for me. He never once called me from work just to hear my voice or send me a message in some way. Never. Our relationship died that day. My mother banished me and so did my father and my brother.

My seven bad years had started.

I went through hell and not one of my family members even wanted to know what happened to me. A lot of what I went through hurt like crazy; my mother throwing my out, my brother too busy with his own life to even think about me, my old friends refusing to be by my side.

Kobi, later on, tore my heart into shreds.

But the greatest pain of all, the pain that would never truly heal, that brings tears to my eyes again even now as eighteen years later I write about it, was the betrayal of my father choosing not to protect me, choosing not to stand up for me, never looking for me, not FIGHTING for me.

That was the day 'his little princess' died forever. And the girl who emerged never believed any man who called her 'his princess' ever again.

But with every death, something new begins. For me, it was a new life. The life of a warrior, of a survivor. The life of a young woman no one fought for, who had to become her own heroine.

This is exactly how the real me was born.

Chapter 03
ALONE

"It is not good that the man should be alone; I will make
him an help meet for him"

(Genesis, 2:18)

When I left my parents' house, I had no idea that my whole life would turn upside down.

From that moment on I was totally alone and eight of the worst years of my life began. Until the military, I was mama's girl. I stayed home to clean, I watched movies and had long walks on the beach with my dad. I was very attached to my parents and brother and couldn't bear a day without them.

I also was very codependent. I never washed dishes or cooked as my mother wouldn't allow anyone in the kitchen. I never went shopping, I never handled money, I never worked except for teaching private lessons to students who were weaker than me. All of a sudden I was on the streets with no idea what to do or even how to get through one single day.

I called Kobi immediately. After all, he was the one I 'chose' over my family. Kobi lived alone but had no intention of letting me stay with him. He explained it might make things worse (for me), but the truth was he wasn't ready for that kind of responsibility and relationship - and I was too naive to see that back then.

I tried calling a few friends, but most of them were away or didn't want to get involved. I felt 'bald from both sides'. I left my parents' house to be with the man I loved and he wouldn't take me in. I had nowhere to go and so I sat on a bench in the park, cried my heart out and tried to call every person I knew. Hours passed and no one came to rescue me.

I was just about to prepare my bed on the bench when my friend Dan called.

"Hey babe, you can stay at Eldar's place."

Eldar was his friend, and had a huge crush on me. I had no choice. I agreed and Eldar came to pick me up. He settled me in his room where he had one tiny bed and so I had to sleep next to him, feeling extremely uncomfortable.

Of course he expected something in return. I could feel his breath on my neck and he cuddled closer to me. Way too close. I pretended to not feel it and to be asleep.

I could barely sleep a couple of hours but the next day he went to work and I had time alone. I kept calling every person I knew. I finally reached my friend Ruth's house. Her mother answered, and I started explaining what happened, crying my heart out. She listened and told me to come over.

"You can stay here. Ruth just signed up to the Lieutenants' military course, she won't be home much and you can take her room."

Her name was Ilana. And for years to come she was my saviour.

The most important thing Ilana did was that she didn't judge me.

For her, I wasn't a slut, a stupid girl, blinded by love or naive or whatever. I was just me and I was still to discover myself, to explore how I felt and become who I wanted to become. She would listen to me for hours and encourage me to stop feeling so much guilt and shame. You see, I was feeling like the worst daughter in the world. Like someone who couldn't be loved unconditionally - even by her own family.

I felt like a bad girlfriend since my boyfriend didn't want me around. But Ilana loved having me around. And I had a roof, I had food, I had someone who cared about me.

It didn't last forever, of course. A few months later, Ruth finished her course and wanted her mother 'back' so I had to leave.

But by that time I'd found a job and a little apartment to rent. It was an awful apartment, with cockroaches and a mattress on the floor, but for the first time in my life I was independent.

I cooked my own food (I burnt almost everything), I came and went as I wished, I answered no one's orders or questions. The only problem was that I was lonely. I'd never, ever been lonely before in my life.

In the meantime, Kobi had developed an ugly habit of coming and going in my life as he pleased.

He wanted no responsibility, he had a thousand excuses and I was far too desperate for his attention and love.

He would spend a few days, maybe a week, with me and then would leave with the excuse that I was too much, or too little, too young, too beautiful, he had second thoughts about his ex-wife, he needed to go on a business trip, he was sick, he was scared, he was...whatever.

I accepted all his excuses with love and tried to be the best girlfriend I could be. My parents and I would rarely communicate and when we did it would only involve shouting, fighting and then ignoring each other.

My mother would go to any friend or landlord I had and convince them they were destroying a family by helping me.

So I was often evicted, isolated from friends, ending up crying on the streets or at Ilana's place, once again having to find an apartment. I tried to ask Kobi for help but he was never ready to do anything.

I couldn't sleep. I couldn't hold down a job and I had very little money to live on. I started eating potatoes and drinking vodka - that was what my budget allowed and the vodka helped me to sleep.

I was constantly filled with guilt and shame. No one really loved me. Not even Ilana, not as much as she loved her daughter, anyway.

The loneliness was horrible, but the worst of it came at night. I could hear every cricket, every bird, and the darkness scared me. I felt totally alone.

I told myself I could die and nobody would even notice. I felt the loneliness like a hand of cold steel grabbing my guts. It was cruel, it was merciless. I couldn't stand it!

As it got so much worse at night and I couldn't sleep anyway, I started going out in the darkness and walking the streets. I didn't care what might happen to me. Sometimes I'd walk to Kobi's house to see what he was doing that meant he didn't want me around.

He was usually not home so I would climb up to look through the windows and feel even worse about myself.

Sometimes I would walk to my parents' house and wonder how could they give up on me so easily and the feeling of guilt would increase. I would imagine my mother cleaning the house all by herself without me to help her and I felt so sorry.

But I couldn't go back to them because that meant giving up on the shreds of love and attention that Kobi gave me. And most of all it meant I would be admitting defeat and swallowing my pride.

So I walked all night long. Many times I was harassed, picked up by bored truckers or taxi drivers and I stayed with them all night long. I didn't care where, I just couldn't bear being alone. Alone with me.

In all this time one thing never changed - my daily training. The one gift my father gave me that saved my life. Teaching me to weightlift. I always found a way to train. I always found a few pennies for the gym as it was more important than food for me. When I was in the gym I was strong. Life outside the gym didn't matter. It was me and the bar. The weights. The determination. I could lift this, I could push this, I was strong, I was invincible!

Regardless of all the shit and suffering in my life, during that sacred time when I was between those walls it felt like I had hundreds of friends in the weights themselves. I accomplished my goals and I was who I wanted to be instead of the starving, pathetic, lonely, hated girl I was in the outside world.

It was a feeling that deepened and deepened every single day with the cold shoulder from my parents and the constant abandonment of Kobi. I was a wreck.

I tried once to call my father at work. But his reaction broke my heart. His voice was dry, cold and disinterested.

He said he was busy and that was it. He never tried to call me or ask me if I was okay. My mother became my sworn enemy. Today, I know she was doing her best to protect me but at the time she just seemed to want to destroy me.

I couldn't trust my friends. They would tell her everything about me. She did all she could to destroy Kobi's life - accusations to the Police, calling his ex-wife and talking about me, showing up wherever he was and threatening him to try to get him to leave me alone.

Would I have done the same? Probably not. But she did what she thought would protect me.

But you see, through all that torture, life always sent me solutions. I had no idea at the time, but looking back I know there were books, courses, signs and opportunities. When I didn't see it, when I was sinking into victimhood and my 'poor me' bubble, when I got too used to tears pouring down all the time, life would send me Angels.

Remember Eldar, who saved me the first night from the streets?

Remember Ilana, who saved me for months later?

Now here comes a big one, Alex. Who saved me from dying.

I met Alex when I was walking on the beach. I walked every day in the hope that I might see my father. In some ways, I dreaded seeing him but I continued to do it because it was what we used to do together.

I would walk with stones in my fists, like he taught me, to protect myself in case I was attacked. I would listen to my music and let the sun kiss my skin. I would cry if I wanted to and talk to the sea if I wanted to. The beach was mine, just like the gym.

One day I changed my route and I started to see a familiar face every day. A silver haired man with a gentle look in his eyes.

We started greeting each other until one day, I was walking along crying.

When Alex saw me he said, "Come on, let's walk together."

I started telling him what I was going through. He listened patiently and then told me I should come visit him in his clinic.

Alex was one of the best Psychologists in Israel but I didn't know that at the time. I explained I was too poor to afford help and he said he would not take any money.

I had nothing to lose. I went to see him on our scheduled day. When I arrived my eyes were red from crying and the constant lack of sleep. At the time I hadn't slept for weeks and I'd lost 8kg in a month. I started begging for sleeping pills.

"I can't take it any longer!" I said.

He handed me a box of tissues.

"I am not a Psychiatrist, I don't give medicine. But I will tell you this. If after three meetings you still need a sleeping pill, I'll write you a prescription."

That was a great trick.

I was immediately committed to those three meetings, not believing there was any way I could manage to sleep without help, so I gave him my word and he asked me to tell him why couldn't sleep.

So I talked. I think I talked for three hours without stopping. But once I started talking, I couldn't stop crying. The box of tissues in my lap emptied completely and I had to wipe my face with my shirt, which was completely soaked by the time I managed to stop and take a breath.

Alex only listened. He sat back, his index fingers touching, and listened. Then he picked up a small, black notebook.

He asked me gently, "When could you come again? I would love to listen more but I have another appointment soon - and I need to get more tissues."

We settled a date. I walked back to my cockroach infested apartment. I was feeling light, emptied and relieved. And that night I slept for the first time in a long time.

Alex was right. I didn't need any pill or magic potion. But I needed to talk. I needed someone to see my life from the outside and release the burden of guilt from my shoulders.

Alex and I kept meeting for years. He was always patient, generous with his time and insightful. I always felt light after seeing him.

When he lifted the load from my shoulders, telling me, for example, I shouldn't feel guilty for leaving my parents' house, or for not 'being there' for my mother, I believed him. I started feeling less shame and started seeing right from wrong.

You see, my mother did everything for us at home and wouldn't let us cook, do our dishes, go shopping for groceries, spend our allowance money and so on. The lack of independence and freedom was like a cocoon that sheltered me and protected me from the outside world, but it also closed me off from reality.

I didn't have sleepovers as a child, I didn't make many mistakes or take many risks. I believed in my parents wholeheartedly. Their word was sacred. I never doubted them for a minute. If they said this is good and this is bad - so it was. If they said I was bad, so I was. If they didn't love me enough - then I wasn't worthy. And so on.

The idea that they were wrong was wrong for me! But there was also a lot of confusion in my head. Am I Jewish? Christian? Catholic? Atheist? Is there even a God?

Am I a slut for wanting to have sex with my boyfriend, like my mother said, or normal, like my boyfriend said?

If I am not a good daughter, am I a bad person? My questions were endless. And Alex had the answers.

I started learning about my life, about God, about right and wrong.

I found a job I actually liked and a better apartment. I could sleep. I finally learned to cook for myself. I started reading again and taking care of myself. I made some new friends. I started forgiving myself.

I found and adopted a kitten and I wasn't so lonely anymore. I loved that little creature with all my heart and I knew she would never hurt me.

I started gaining control over my life and the cold-steel lonely feeling started to ease.

But there were two major issues that were constantly painful and stopped me from feeling happy or free.

These things stopped me from becoming who I was meant to be and they constantly caused me to take two steps back every time I took one step forward.

What do you think they were? My family, of course. And Kobi.

Chapter 04
REVENGE

"For love is as strong as death; jealousy is as cruel as
the grave"

(Song Of Solomon, 8:6)

While my brother was completing his military service we drifted further and further apart until we never really spoke. I missed him terribly but I was also hurt that he didn't try to contact me to ask how I was doing.

I always felt that my parents preferred him over me and I suspected that now that I was the 'bad apple' in the family, their bond as a unit of three had grown.

I felt isolated and betrayed by them all. I was almost grateful, at times, for my mother's spying on me and her habit of interfering in everything she could, as it meant that on some level she still cared.

I started seeing obsessed, needy behaviour as a sign of love and started using this strategy for myself. My mother would follow me whenever she could. She visited my homes and workplaces. She talked to everyone and turned people against me - the famous tactic of 'defer and rule'. As the years passed, her behaviour was consistent and worse every time.

Subconsciously, I copied it.

Kobi would disappear and leave me on a regular basis. The constant heartbreak and disappointment hit me every time. When he returned my hopes would rise simply to be shattered in pieces after a few days.

The constant abandonment and rejection I felt from both Kobi and my family turned a sweet, innocent girl into a bitter, needy, crazy monster.

I started following him, talking to people about him, calling him and buying him presents to convince him to be with me. I would sleep on his door mat when he disappeared to be there when returned, which he never did. As a Policeman, he knew how to disappear without a trace. I became my mother.

When I started talking to Alex he pointed this out to me. He pointed out how toxic my relationship with Kobi was as the one with my mother. He told me that he couldn't discern between those relationships.

But I needed to get stronger before I could make a decision, or so I thought. Today I know it is the opposite - decision making makes you stronger. There is no 'right moment' to make a decision.

To the outside world I was a mystery. I was crazy, needy, isolated, angry, sassy, daring. I was a very clever and very sexy young woman.

I started realising my sexual power in the military, but that was all I realised about it - the power. I used this power to manipulate people - to get a job, to get a free ride, to get food, to get a discount.

But on a deeper level I was using my power in order to avoid being alone. I didn't enjoy any of the sex I had. In fact, I never climaxed. It was all a power game for me.

With Kobi the sex was terrible. That is something I'd have to revisit later in life - my willingness to compromise who I am.

But at the time, I didn't know it was so bad. I didn't know it could be better. I never enjoyed sex anyway. I was convinced I had a problem. And since I didn't want to seem like a little girl or a freak, I faked it. I said it was great, I acted as if it was amazing. I was loyal and giving and as undemanding as possible.

When he left me, I stayed home, lit candles and prayed for his return. I would write letters to God asking him to bring him back, cried myself to sleep, skipped work and refused to go out with the few friends I managed to make.

I would spend all my money on fortune tellers to try to understand why he didn't love me enough to commit and to ask what could I do to change it. It drove me crazy.

I would stay awake for nights waiting to hear his knock on the door, which would follow by his voice telling me he missed me, he needs me, he loves me. That knock always came,eventually. But that knock ruined my life.

I couldn't move forward as I just waited for the knock, sometimes for months at a time, wasting my youth on someone who just saw me as a toy.

To cheer myself up after the first few days of 'mourning' his loss I would do my hair, put some makeup on, wear my most revealing clothes and go out on the town. The attention I received from men was encouraging. I started enjoying it more and more and then started to take numbers for 'lonely times' instead of saying that I had a boyfriend.

When lonely times came, I made a phone call or two. At the beginning it was just to go out for coffee or a drink, to ease the pain of rejection and loneliness.

I would think to myself, "Now then, Kobi. You see. Even when you don't want me, others do!"

I would hope to be seen going out with those men so that he would hear about it and feel jealous.

But going out didn't do the trick. The loneliness crept back in. I needed more power, I hated being alone. So from a drink, it became a kiss, it became making out, it became leaving the guy wanting more while I had the power. And it felt good.

The lonely nights became much more interesting and much more sexy.

As I started going out more and more I spotted one of Kobi's friends in a club checking me out. I enjoyed the attention. I wanted him to tell Kobi he saw me and that I looked great. So I went over to him and asked him to do so. I gave him my number and asked if he could let me know Kobi's reaction. And so he did.

His name was Avi. He was a big guy with bright blue eyes. He had the look of a man who knew his ways with women.

He called me the next day and told me that Kobi had his 'poker face' on but said that he could see it affected him. Then he asked me why I'd be so hung up on a man who was so much older than me and who didn't appreciate me. We started talking and he invited me out for a drink.

That drink became the first time in my life I enjoyed sex.

It seemed to me that Avi had an electricity field around him. When he laid his eyes on me I could feel electricity running through my body. I couldn't resist but, then again, why should I?

We had the first good sex of my life and I was blown away. What a way to spend my 'waiting time'!

We started meeting regularly and things became more and more intense as he started telling me Kobi had other women. It turned out that Kobi was using me for an ego boost and his interest in me was not serious.

Whether that was true or not, I fell into the trap. My anger and determination to taste revenge grew by the minute. When Kobi called Avi while we were having sex and I felt pride instead of shame.

"Now there you go, you asshole!" I thought to myself.

In my fantasy world Avi would fall madly in love with me and both men would fight to have me in their lives.

But this fantasy was about to blow up in my face in a very ugly way.

At the time, I was working six different jobs to pay for my rent and food. I also signed up for a student loan and decided to start studying for a degree in Psychology and Criminology.

I was a ball of energy - working, studing for my University entrance exams and having sex with Avi whenever I could. My late evening job was in a bar cafe in the city. I took a late night shift so I could study in the morning and juggle other work.

The late night shift was charged with sexual energy. And I loved every minute of it. Avi started coming to the bar in the last few minutes of my shift. We'd enjoy a glass of wine together and he'd take me home.

One day he turned up with a friend, who I later learned was Kobi's commander in the police. I was feeling on top of my world. There I was, finishing an eight hour shift at 3am with two handsome men sitting there just waiting for a chance to be with me.

I am not alone, I am not unwanted, I am not unloved. I can get anyone! That was how I felt.

One night, Avi needed to leave but the commander stayed. We drank our nightcap sitting on the rocks at the border with Lebanon. But I felt lonely and tears started running down my cheeks.

This was a place I'd always wanted to sit with Kobi. But instead, here I was with a stranger and a glass of wine. The commander saw my tears. He hugged me and said that nobody is worth my tears - especially not Kobi.

He told me about a time he'd been to Kobi's apartment for a drink and when he arrived Kobi was there with a woman in the bedroom.

When he knocked, Kobi invited him to 'join them'. But when he refused, Kobi 'finished the deal', left the bedroom and said "She's all ready for you now."

I couldn't bear the pain.

Why would he betray me like that? I was in my twenties, beautiful, smart and free! Why would he disappear on me to be with another woman twice my age? The only explanation was, as usual, that I wasn't good enough. Not for him, not for my family, not for anyone. The tears were like burning fire in my throat and my stomach. I couldn't bear it. I just couldn't!

I turned to the commander and kissed him. Then I asked him to take me home. I invited him in and had sex with him. It was horrible and I knew it was wrong. He was married, he was Kobi's commander and Avi's friend.

But there was nothing worse than the cold-steel of loneliness, accompanied by the feeling, or should I say, the knowledge that nobody wanted me.

I told Alex everything. He never judged. He listened. He explained. He told me that this man I had in my life was toxic for me and that I needed to get away.

But I couldn't take his advice. I spilled my heart out on his sofa time after time yet went back to my life full of mistakes, self-sabotage and hate.

I started having sex every day with Avi and the commander, juggling my time, not telling one about the other.

When Kobi returned I'd silence my phone and be with him. I had sex with him feeling satisfied by the idea that he was inside me just a few hours after both his friends had been, and that he didn't know it.

Soon, the two men weren't enough to fulfill my growing hunger for power, control and revenge.

Nothing could satisfy my hunger. The black hole within me was growing minute by minute.

So I started having sex with every guy I liked. I was shameless, I was ruthless.

I also became numb again. I stopped enjoying the sex, it was just a power game. I needed to be on top. I needed to feel in control. I needed to humiliate men, to make them obey me, to spit at them, slap them and torture them with desire.

I wanted them to beg me. But most of all, I wanted them to never leave me. Often I broke into pieces after a fake climax and begged them not to leave me, not to stop loving me.

These random men wouldn't understand what had happened to the badass woman riding them minutes before. They always left. And the black hole inside me grew bigger every time.

Despite the price I paid of the pain that would come after these sexual encounters, this was how I spent my time.

Anything was better than constant loneliness and rejection. One night when no one could come to my bed, I ordered an escort.

Anything was better than being alone.

Then one day it all exploded.

Kobi had an argument with Avi and said something hurtful. Avi responded he'd been fucking his girlfriend and it all came out. Kobi exploded into my small apartment furious and in tears. He started breaking everything he could find until he found my diary. He sat down and read it.

I sat down beside him, not knowing what to do or what to expect.

I wanted him to know but I'd dreaded this moment and I started to realise how bad this could all become. It was all written down. All the men, all the sex, all my revenge.

He took out his gun and pointed it at me.

"You make me crazy! How could you do this to me?" he said.

Shaking and crying, he then turned the gun on himself and opened his mouth.

"You make me want to die!" he said, and shoved it in.

I broke into hysterical tears. I took the gun and turned it back on myself.

I went down on my knees and cried.

"Please, please don't do this. I am begging you. I am not worth it. I am a whore, I should be punished, not you. I love you!"

He looked at me, and said, "Don't you move anywhere."

He took my phone, broke it to pieces and walked out.

My landlord was outside the door waiting for an explanation about the shouting, the crashing sounds and the drama.

I tried to explain, but he was tired of the scenes, of the men and of my mother coming constantly to ask questions.

"You need to leave. You have three days."

I was lost. I had no phone. I had to leave my apartment. I had to keep my jobs. I had just started University. And I had no idea what was going on with Kobi.

Again, I was alone. And again, I felt I deserved it. I was worth nothing and that was all I had.

Chapter 05
PRISON BREAK

"Keep me from my lovers, and I will keep
me from my haters"

(Voltaire, inspired by King David's
discussions with God)

For the next two years I was a prisoner.

I somehow managed to find another apartment and made friends with a gentle old man called Tom.

He was my only friend, the only friend I could have. Kobi kept me under his watch at all times. I would go to University, then go to work, then come home. He refused to live with me but he would ambush me with surprise visits. At work, in my new apartment, even at University.

The only thing was that he didn't disappear out of my life so often. I would wake up to see him staring intensely at me with his eyes full of anger and sadness.

I felt so much shame and guilt. I was a slut, I was worse than a prostitute because I'd had all that sex for free.

I didn't understand why I did what I did and I didn't blame anyone for it but myself. The whole town spoke about me and how many men I'd slept with. I was fired from my job and I had no friends but Tom. I had to lie to him about Kobi in order for him to think well of me.

I'd humiliated Kobi. Although I wasn't with him, in his opinion, I was still expected to be loyal.

I felt disgusting. My idea about sex had changed again. This time I became like a complete nun. I let no one flirt with me. I went through university with no social life and no sex except the guilty sex I had with Kobi.

He was allowed to offend me, humiliate me and treat me as he wished because I was nothing but a whore.

I couldn't talk to anyone about it. And I couldn't see Alex any longer because Kobi wouldn't allow it. I suffered in silence for two years. I was living in a prison I created for myself.

I graduated from University, which was a surprise considering my circumstances. Despite the poverty, the lack of support and my lack of self care I was still top of my class. My teachers thought I was brilliant. If only they'd known how brilliant I could really be if I wasn't living a life of hell!

When I graduated, I was the only one in the university with nobody in the crowd waiting for her.

My parents refused to come to what they believed was a fake ceremony. And my boyfriend was away working. I was alone after achieving so much and coming top in everything. I felt no pride or joy. I didn't even celebrate. After all, why would I celebrate the life I was living?

As time passed, I started feeling like I'd paid the price for my choices. After two years of living as a prisoner without an ounce of freedom, humiliated in every possible moment, I decided that enough was enough.

I kept thinking about what my favourite teacher, Prof. Silfan, used to tell me during Criminology class. He said there was only one reason for a woman not to leave an abusive relationship and that is that 'she didn't have enough'.

Back then I felt very angry when he said that but I realised he was right. I didn't have 'enough', as I wasn't 'enough'! I didn't have enough shame, enough humiliation, enough punishment. I didn't have enough to make me want to leave. I didn't have enough to draw the line.

I also didn't have enough because the more I stayed, the more comfortable I became with the evil I knew. The more my boundaries and pain level were tested and stretched.

But when I graduated with two degrees in half the usual time, I felt like I was done paying the price. I decided I had been punished enough. I believed I had learned enough. It was time to turn a page.

I found a job as a social worker, helping mentally disabled people. It was a poorly paid job but at least I was recognised for my brains this time. It was a fascinating, yet sometimes dangerous, job and it made me realise how lucky I actually was.

I woke up to the fact that I still wanted to live my life.

I went to the bank and took out another loan. This time I signed up to the Wingate Institute gym instructors course. It was a six month course and I was able to work in a gym after three months. I could manage my job while doing something I loved with all my heart.

For the first time in years, I felt excited. I couldn't wait.

My prison sentence was over. Life was smiling at me again - I was smiling again! A new chapter was about to begin for me, free of guilt and free of shame. I had paid enough.

Conveniently, Kobi had to leave the area to work for a while. I was literally FREE.

The morning I began my course I wore my best clothes. I hitch hiked to the city and, when the course started, I adored every second of it - the people, the tutor, the books.

I loved learning anatomy and physiology, the science behind everything and I loved the coffee breaks we had in the beautiful cafe downstairs. I was in love. And I was such a great student that, a month later, the tutor singled me out as a 'rising star' and offered me a job in one of the collaborative gyms.

Oh my God! Doing what I love - and getting paid for it! Life was good.

I worked, studied and made friends. I was happy. From time to time Kobi returned for a break and would look for me, but I was already in a much better place and his visits didn't destroy me any more.

For the first time in my life I understood how talented I was and how it was important it is for my soul to work in a place where I could feel appreciated and love what I do. I started feeling stronger again, physically and mentally.

I passed the course with flying colours and achieved the diploma that meant I could work wherever I desired.

I started working in three or four gyms, met so many people and thoroughly enjoyed my life.

I lived in a small, one room apartment with my cat. I got along with my landlord - a warm, religious woman who shared her delicious food with me.

In the meantime, my parents relocated to Italy for my father's work and I was free of that stress too. I never stopped missing them, especially now that I had more space from Kobi, but the fresh air in my life was intoxicating and I enjoyed it fully.

While Kobi was away, I started going out with my new friends and occasionally went on a date with someone interesting. My heart still belonged to him but I started to realise that I was worth more than constant abandonment. I deserved better than to be treated like trash.

Everything seemed to be going well...until the war started.

Chapter 06
BLOOD, SWEAT AND TEARS

"When I walk in the valley of the shadow of death, I
fear no harm, because you are with me"

(Psalm 23:14)

It seemed like a normal morning. As I never watched the news, I had no idea what was going on.

But at 6am I was in the bathroom brushing my teeth, when I heard a loud boom and the window near me shattered all over my shoulder.

I thought it must be a ball from kids playing outside in the school yard next to where I lived, plucked the glass out of my shoulder and kept getting ready for work.

Soon enough there were anxious knocks on my door.

"Mirav! Mirav! Are you in there? Get out! Come to the shelter!"

It was my landlord.

The city I lived in was on the Lebanese border, so even the sirens couldn't warn us in time. What had exploded next to me and broke the window into my shoulder was a Katyusha bomb sent from Lebanon, not a ball.

The war had begun.

I grabbed my cat and my cell phone and ran, in pyjamas and bare feet, to the shelter. Just in time, as we rushed inside, we could hear bombs exploding one after another. They were so close by that it seemed as if they were landing right on top of us and that any second the shelter would collapse.

I hate fireworks, even today, because they sound exactly the same.

My cat was terrified. I was sweating with anxiety.

We turned on the TV - luckily, in Israel, our shelters are maintained like 'second homes' underground.

They have to be clean and equipped with food, bedding, medicine and first aid at all times, as well as landline telephone and a television for news broadcasts.

We could see what was happening with the bombs exploding in my city.

"Attacks on Nahariya!" it said.

The Hizbullah (a Lebanese terror organisation) took responsibility for the bombing. They wanted four hundred terrorist prisoners to be released so that they could return to their killer forces. Until then, their intention was to make our lives a misery.

And so they did.

For six weeks we remained underground, receiving food from the police help units, visited by ambulances checking for 'anxiety injuries' while they collected physical casualties.

At the time I didn't realize I was, indeed, suffering from anxiety too and that that war would leave scars on my soul for the rest of my life.

Although I wasn't physically injured, the constant fear, the death around me, the screams, the sirens, the smoke, my city in flames, the abandoned houses and lives - it was enough.

I struggled with living underground, starved of fresh air and freedom. I used to always be outside, always looking for things to do. I missed my walks on the beach. I missed looking at a sky free from smoke. I missed feeling safe. I was so scared that I'd miss hearing a bomb approaching when I was in the shower that I stopped showering alone.

I was sure a bomb was destined to destroy our shelter.

After a few nights, my landlord asked me to find a different shelter because she wasn't comfortable with having me around. They were a religious family and I was a young girl, 'hardly dressed'.

It was August in Israel and the thought of being enclosed in the hot shelter with long religious robes on was tortuous, but I offered to do it. After all, where would I go?

But my landlord refused to let me stay and I had to sleep outside of the shelter at night. Well, I couldn't sleep. I was sure I would 'wake up dead' (*note to reader - humor always was a life saver in my worst situations in life!)

Most of the city's residents had left. Many had fled the country. Buildings were destroyed by bombs, local thieves had looted shops and houses like wild animals over dead bodies.

I had only one friend left in town and she wasn't afraid of the bombs at all.

"If we are supposed to die, we shall. If not, there is nothing to worry about," she said.

So I spent the rest of the war with her, hiding in her 'shelter' - her positive, life loving attitude.

When I heard bombs I would hold her tight until they passed.

"If I die, at least I won't die alone," I thought.

We even made a joke about putting extra effort into doing our makeup and wearing matching underwear in the morning, although we hardly even went out of the house, saying the Hizbullah wouldn't kill us if we looked hot, and if they did the meds will be 'fighting over our bodies' (literally) to save our lives.

That joke put a smile on my face and a reason to stay human, despite the inhumane shit going on. It was a wake up, put on some makeup and nice clothes, do your hair like you don't care kind of thing.

My friend's positivity, her way of daring life and her belief that death and destiny are 'written' were contagious.

I can't describe the fear in words. The Hizbullah had no respect for international laws, which require them to pause bombing to allow people to leave their shelters to get food or visit hospitals. They would drop bombs at all times of the day and night.

Things got worse day by day. I lost all my jobs because I was unable to travel. The bank continued to take payments for my university loan, but no money came in. So day by day I sunk further and further into debt.

I would look at my beloved to-do lists, the lists that always made me feel in control of my life, the lists that supported me to find an apartment, to find a job, to achieve my goals, to get jobs done. But all my lists were now useless.

I couldn't do a single thing and anything I'd planned to do on the day the war started was delayed until further notice.

I made an official promise to myself, then and there, to never delay what I can do today until tomorrow.

Life can end any minute.

I vowed to enjoy life more, to say 'yes' more, to have more fun and to do more every day I'm alive.

I've kept this promise to this very day.

Yes, there may be things I will delay or postpone, but these would never be things I'd consider to be top priority.

The war turned me into a productive, Action Queen!

This fact, and my passion for life, were the war's blessings.

As the weeks passed, it seemed the war would never end.

I started going out as soon as the bombs stopped. I took my bike and I rode to the gym although everything was broken, burnt and black. But I sat on a bench anyway and I started training.

A few minutes later, another guy must have had the same thought and turned up at the gym. There we were, the two of us, between ashes and black mirrors, lifting dumbells and laughing at how ridiculous we'd look to the Hizbullah watching us, keeping our bodies in shape so we could 'die beautiful'.

It was so good to laugh!

When the bombs began again, the strength I'd got from training and laughing had soaked right into my cells and for the first time, I felt myself pushing the fear away.

We watched the bombs fall from the balcony of the ruined gym, saying prayers for the people who were about to get hurt or die, wishing this would all finally stop.

I was daring enough to cycle to visit a dear friend who wasn't able to leave the town. She was one of my angels, Miriam.

She was a woman who'd been through a bigger hell than I had, yet never lost the smile from her face. She always had a plate of food for me and she offered the best advice I could ever wish for.

For seven years she listened to my endless stories, wiped my tears and loved me as if I was her own daughter.

"You always need to put yourself first, Mirav," she would say, while I would sip her amazing coffee and we would watch Spanish soap operas together.

"Stop giving so much thought and effort to this Kobi guy. He is really not worth it. Stop feeling guilty about your parents. Stop cutting yourself into the smallest pieces and feeding them to others, pleasing others and leaving yourself with nothing. It's YOU who comes first. Even when you have children one day.

You. You. You.

Then your children. Then everyone else...."

Her words lingered in my head for years to come, slowly sinking in until I finally understood their full meaning, 15 years after hearing them.

Miriam was one of the wisest women I've ever known, yet she'd not even had the opportunity to finish school. She was a single mother for many years, and with just her two hard working hands she took care of her blind mother and raised four children all alone.

She was one of the greatest mentors I ever had.

Empowered by my newly found courage, I cycled to see her. Bombs started falling as I pedalled. I didn't know what to do or where to hide, so I just kept cycling, missing some of the bombs by just 40 meters.

I arrived at her home and ran into the shelter. There she was, my angel, with her warm cup of coffee. She was comforting her young son, who was shaking as one of the guys went out of the shelter for a smoke, and a bomb blew off his head. We sat together and talked for hours until the bombs stopped and I cycled back to my makeshift home.

My escapes became a daily occurence. I'd take my bicycle and ride to the gym, to see Miriam, or to the hospital where I'd volunteer.

Doing nothing all day long, feeling so scared of the bombs and the experience of my life being on hold was driving me crazy.

My parents were living in South Italy because of my father's UN mission. They didn't seem to worry too much that I couldn't fly over to be with them because the airports were closed.

One day Kobi called, and came to collect me on his motorbike.

"Don't worry, nothing will happen to you when you are with me," he said.

I needed that reassurance. I needed to feel safe. And I really needed to connect with someone.

As I held tightly onto him, sitting on the back of his motorcycle, the bombs started again. There was fire everywhere and he steered the bike in a slalom, avoiding the bombs by the skin of his teeth. I couldn't stand it - there was fire everywhere, noises, smoke. I buried my face in his back and just prayed it would all be over.

We arrived at his place and, for that weekend, it felt like there was no war. We ate, laughed and watched movies. The bombs and the war seemed so far away, but that was just an illusion.

As the week began, Kobi took me back. When I begged to stay with him in his safe, cosy home he said he had work and he couldn't leave me in the house alone. He left, disappearing again from my life.

Once again nobody really cared about what was happening or what might happen to me - not him, not my family, no one.

Back in the war zone my daily escapes were not enough any longer, once I'd enjoyed a weekend of freedom. I missed my beach, my daily walks, the feeling of the sun on my skin and the taste of salt in the air.

So I decided "Screw it. If I need to die, I will."

I waited until the bombs stopped; usually there would be a few hours breaks in between the attacks, and between 2pm and 6pm it seemed to be relatively quiet. I used to laugh and say the Hizbullah are having their siesta. I put on my trainers, grabbed my favourite music and went to the beach.

On my way I called the Police to ask if there were any alerts.

"None," they reassured me, "but we still recommend you stay in the shelters."

"Too late," I thought with a smile.

Ah...my beach. The smell of the sea instead of the stench of smoke, the touch of the sun's rays instead of the unbearable heat of shelters and the smell of everyone's sweat.

I started walking briskly and looked at the sky with gratitude.

"Thank you God, for letting me do this," I said.

Glancing back, I looked over towards the Lebanese border. All of a sudden I noticed that smoke was rising.

Holy shit! This was meant to be official rest time - there were not supposed to be any bombs and the police had said there were no alerts!

But my eyes didn't fool me. I was only five miles away from Lebanon and this was the perfect range to be hit right in the face from that Katyusha.

Shit, shit, what do I do? What did they say on TV to do if you are caught outside?

I looked behind me - there was a fuel station. Shit. If that explodes I'm going to turn into crisp meat. I looked towards the sea. Should I jump in the water?

While all this was going through my head, a bomb was launched. I could see it above my head, such an ugly machine created to take lives. It landed in the water.

That was a sign for me. I started walking forwards, thinking that the closer I got to the border the less likely it would be that I'd die because the Hizbullah wouldn't bomb themselves.

But by now bombs were being constantly launched. One after another. One landed in the fuel station behind me and the explosion was deafening. I was in shock. I broke out in a cold sweat and started shaking like a leaf.

"There's nothing else to do. I might die. I might live. I'd better not move."

So I dropped down onto the hot sand and buried my face in the dry herbs. I kept hearing bombs above me and each bomb seemed like the one which was sent to take my life away.

"When I walk in the valley of the shadow of death, I fear no harm, because you are with me." I started whispering to myself, again and again and again.

Ever since my military service this had been my favourite phrase. We were sworn in with it and it was used in the funerals of the soldiers who'd given their lives for our country.

The fact that my favourite song in those days, Gangster's Paradise, started with that quote was no coincidence.

"When I walk in the valley of the shadow of death, I fear no harm, because you are with me" I kept whispering again and again, my face buried in the sand, waiting for the bombs to stop.

"Shma Israel Adonai Eloheinu Adonai Ehad"

"Listen, Israel, God is our God and God is One" I added from time to time, my eyes closed tightly and my hands clasped together. I heard this sentence saved thousands of lives.

"Dear God, please keep me alive today. I swear if you do, once the war is over, I'll tattoo this on my left arm, in your honor." I thought, between my whispers.

I lost all sense of time. I could have been there for five minutes or five hours. I'll never know.

But suddenly I heard ambulances and police sirens. That meant the bombs had stopped and they were on their way to find and help the casualties.

In my relief, I stood up and walked towards the sound of the sirens.

I was shaking and scared. I couldn't even talk clearly.

"I have an anxiety injury," I said to one of the Police Officers. "Could any of you escort me home please?"

But they refused. They were too busy rescuing severely injured people.

A truck of reporters stopped nearby and I walked towards them, shaking.

"Could you please drop me home?"

"Sure," they answered. It was great for them to have a picture of me, sitting in the back of their truck, shaking and in shock.

I finally arrived at my friend's shelter. My courageous moments were over. I didn't leave the apartment again. Food had lost its taste, I was too scared to shower and sleep became a fantasy.

A week later, the war was over.

I was beyond happy. The world was safe again!

I needed to look for a job, to deal with my growing debts and to return to a normal life.

But first thing's first.

I visited the tattoo artist in Haifa, and fulfilled my promise.

It's my favourite tattoo. It reminds me of how short life is and how important faith can be. It reminds me of my love for my country and my roots and my respect for the soldiers who sacrificed their lives. But most of all it reminds me of the fundamental importance of FREEDOM.

Chapter 07
PEACE

"The wolf also shall dwell with the lamb, and the
leopard shall lie down with the kid"

(Isaia 11:6)

I stayed in Israel for a year after the war.

I broke up with Kobi when I'd finally had enough of his behaviour and nothing he tried would get me back with him.

I found a job in a hotel as a receptionist, I got myself a rebound boyfriend and I was keen to discover what my next step should be.

I couldn't find a better paying job in the city where I lived so I needed to move and begin my life somewhere new. But I had no money. My university and Wingate student loans grew with interest day by day. I couldn't pay my rent any longer so my parents agreed that I could live in their apartment for a while as long as I abided by their rules, which I did.

But my salary wasn't enough to cover my loans, food and basic living costs. Soon the electricity in my apartment was cut off. Debt collectors were constantly knocking on the door. Every cent I earned was swallowed up by the loans and I had no money for food. I signed up for food supplies for the poor and lived on that.

Every passing day it felt like the knocking at my door increased and the pressure to come up with a solution grew.

My rebound boyfriend turned out to be addicted to Marihuana and one day he slapped me. That was the end of our story.

Feeling miserable, scared, lonely, devastated and desperate, I called my parents.

After making sure Kobi was past history, they invited me for a fortnight's holiday at their home in Italy. I jumped on this offer knowing that for a whole two weeks there would be no knocking at the door, I wouldn't be hungry and I didn't have to be scared. There would be light, hot water and a shower!

I knew I'd have to respect my parent's rules but beggars can't be choosers, right? It was a no brainer. So I flew to Italy.

When my feet landed in the beautiful, green fields of South Italy, I felt as if I could breathe for the first time. It was all so green and clean! There were no signs of war, no black walls, no paranoid people cursing in Arabic.

There was no loud techno music and nobody chasing after me with threats over my debts.

It was all so calm and forgiving. Lunch break in Italy was five hours! I only had a fifteen minute lunch break working at the hotel and I worked eight hours on and eight hours off for seven days per week.

And the food! Oh my sweet God, the Italian food was the best!

My parents' apartment was tiny and their rules were annoying. I had no privacy, I slept on a couch and I could hear my mother talking about me to my father every freaking morning while I was supposedly asleep.

But it was still better than the life that was waiting for me in Israel, the memories I had there, the heartache and the hunger.

I met a girl named Anna. She introduced me to her Italian friends. We went out to parties and bars and I danced and sang and drank the life back into me.

My parents were annoyed because I spent so much time with Anna. She fascinated me. She was my first Italian friend. She was beautiful and so well groomed. She did her hair and makeup and was intentional about what she wore each day. I admired that because it was something I hadn't done for so long and it was contagious.

I started looking after myself better and following the example set by my new friend. She was a friend who knew nothing about my previous life, about Kobi, about the war, about the pain.

And then I met Rafael. He was the Romeo of my fantasies. Macho, manly, dark and passionate. And he wanted me! We didn't understand each other at all so we used a pen and paper, drawings and a simple paper vocabulary book I'd brought from Israel.

Rafael started showing me the real Italy. This was the Italy I didn't see with my parents or Anna. I was having the time of my life, listening to Eros Ramazzoti, dancing in underground clubs, eating like I would never eat again.

Rafael took me to the home where he lived with his parents, like most Italians do until they get married, regardless of age. We enjoyed lunches and dinners together, and many liters of local red table wine. I was drunk by everything around me... They were curious about my life and I used the vocabulary book, drawings and my hands to explain it all.

They were excited when I came over to eat and I fell in love with that family. I loved the way they chatted and teased each other. I loved the way they spoiled each other with food and wine and sweets. I loved the way they would all sit on the sofa afterwards and rest, watching football or an Italian comedy and just be together.

I'd never had that in my family and I felt more at home with them then in the apartment with my parents. So I started sleeping at Rafael's. We would enjoy crazy singing and dancing, food, wine, liquers and then we'd have wild sex.

He'd look sad when I'd talk about Israel and the fact that I'd soon be returning there. The sadness in his eyes was the proof I needed to be able to fall in love. I promised to come back and he promised to wait anxiously.

In the meantime, my parents became more and more pissed off. They felt like they'd paid for me to come over for a holiday, not to spend the whole time with new friends, sleeping at a random boy's place.

They didn't see I was already a woman. I'd been through so much during the previous seven years and I was desperate and really fed up. I was sick of that horrible relationship with Kobi, I'd had enough after spending my twenties lighting candles, waiting for him and crying myself to sleep or fucking loads of the wrong guys in order to feel powerful again.

I was fed up of being humiliated, belittled and abused. I was fed up of not being appreciated for my skills, abilities and brain. Fed up of being poor and being chased. Of not being able to have fun. Of having rules and restrictions and conditions everywhere. Fed up of being scared, even if it was the fear of being me.

So I kept on seeing Rafael, spending every moment I could with him, breathing in my freedom and taking all he could give me.

But one day my mother decided to put an end to it and paid Rafael's family a visit.

She told them that I was running away from life in Israel. She told them about my debts and the sad story that I didn't want them to hear. I was rediscovering myself in Italy and I didn't want to drag my past with me, especially not my Mother's version of events.

When she left, Rafael's family were shocked and sad. They were devastated to tell me that my Mother didn't want me visiting them any more and so we'd only be able to meet in secret. They'd never heard anyone speak the way she did about their own daughter so they were surprised and a little suspicious about me.

My mother thought she was setting out the rules and showing

me who was boss. She thought she was saving me from my obsession, running after 'Kobi number two'. But all she achieved was to increase my determination and create yet another drama.

I continued to see Rafael whenever I could, until I had to leave. At our last meeting, Rafael's entire family and I cried like babies - even their rabbit was crying, I think! I swore to return as soon as I could.

And I did. Despite the fact that I paid a very high price to return to Italy, it actually saved my life. Although I didn't realise that fully until ten years later.

Chapter 08
PIVOT

"The end justifies the means"

(Machiavelli)

When I returned to Israel it was even worse than I felt when I'd left. People were running around, there were long crowded lines in the supermarkets, there was constant shouting and cursing in Arabic, nervous drivers…

I couldn't stop comparing Israel to how calm it was in Italy. The streets of my town remained full of war wounds. There were holes in all the buildings and dark grey walls. It was so different from the endless green fields of the 'boot land'.

I returned to my apartment which had no electricity, no TV, not enough food and went straight back to lonely nights after my passionate times with Rafael.

The silence in the apartment was only disturbed by the knocks of the debt collectors, scaring the hell out of me every time, as I hid with my cat in the bathroom. What a contrast it was compared to the joyful clutter of the Italian bars, my parents chatting (even if it was about me!) and the news channel playing in the background without counting bombs, deaths and injuries.

I was a Zionist in my heart and blood, ready to defend my country with my last breath, but I was on my knees with stress.

The war left me with mild PTSD, which was only identified twelve years later when I talked to a coach who recognised my fears and worries as symptoms of trauma.

Every noise startled me; even the whistle of my kettle gave me shivers at times. The sirens and the noises of bombs became an unbearable memory and I also developed claustrophobia. After tasting freedom, I couldn't go back.

Rafael and his family texted me every day, encouraging me to come back, telling me how much they missed me and loved me.

His mother cried on the phone, telling me that I was the daughter she never had. Little did I know at the time that Italians can be very melodramatic and they exaggerate to express their feelings!

But my own parents reverted to giving me the cold shoulder. The bad daughter. The one who used them to come to Italy to chase men and go to nightclubs. I admit, I enjoyed the two week holiday in Italy, I enjoyed the male attention and the clubbing, I enjoyed the food, the calm, the freedom and even my parents' company.

It's just that I could never lay my heart on the table with them. They wouldn't get me and it would always end up in a fight where I would feel frustrated and misunderstood, my mother would blame me for using her and abusing her, and my father would watch it all in silence, then take her side, or any side which wasn't mine, and put in the last evil word.

It could be "Get out", "We don't care about you" or "No wonder you have no friends, no boyfriend, no job..." and I'd feel bad for days, mourning the loss of what I desperately needed and longed for.

I'd also feel really bad about who I am, as if I even knew what that was with all the confusion around me.

So, I tried not to talk too much about anything. But still, whatever I did was always wrong. I just couldn't win.

Rafael's Mother would cry on the phone, "Figlia mia, torni da me..." ("my daughter, come back to me...") and "Mi manchi tanto tanto... troppo..." ("I miss you so much, too much!").

It broke my heart but, in some ways, it healed it too. I was desperate to feel loved and I felt so loved by them. I imagined myself living as part of their family, happily ever after. I had to go back there.

But how?

I found an advert on the internet from an Israeli company in Milan looking for workers. The salary was 1000 Euros a week. They offered training, provided apartments and organised permission to work. They'd take care of you while you lived in their community of Israeli expats in Milan.

Perfect.

Within three months I could repay all my debts in Israel, learn Italian and get all my paperwork to remain in Italy.

All I'd have to do was get there. But I had absolutely no money. I had no job either. I went to the travel agents and they told me the cheapest ticket was 700 Euros. That was 3500 Nis, and I had maybe 50.

But here's the thing about me - when I want something badly enough - I always manage to get it. I wouldn't give up.

So I started looking for fast paying work. I sold all I had - my little car, my gym membership, my clothes. I met a guy in the gym who was looking for a place to stay and I told him he could stay at my place for a few months if he paid me in advance.

I had no right to rent out my parents' apartment, I know, and I paid the price for it later on as did he, but at the time I just really wanted to get back to Italy and I didn't care how.

I bought a simple Italian beginners' course and started studying it. I offered private lessons, cleaning services, babysitting, dog walking - everything I could. The money was still not even close.

Then I found a way to borrow half of the money I needed through the black market. I knew it was dangerous and I could literally lose a leg for it, but relying on the fact that I'd be making so much money in Milan I did it anyway.

Now I was only 1000 Nis (200 Euros) short.

I don't really remember how it happened, but I bumped into Avi, my first lover. We started talking about everything that had gone on. I told him that I hadn't been with Kobi for the last year and everything that had happened since he discovered my betrayal.

Avi told me he'd got engaged but had lost his job, thanks to Kobi. Kobi was so angry with him that he got him fired from the Police force. His character was so ruined that he couldn't even get a security job. He was angry and wanted revenge.

When he learned I needed money he offered me an opportunity - if I'd talk to a local reporter and tell the truth about how he'd been fired, how Kobi had abused and abandoned me and how I'd been affected, it would clear his name, reek the revenge he wanted and allow him to find a job.

I knew it would put Kobi under a bus. Avi didn't just want me to tell the truth, he wanted me to lie, to exaggerate and to describe the whole thing as much worse than it actually was.

He offered me the money I desperately needed and so I agreed to consider it.

For the next two days I was tempted. I needed the money and Kobi had destroyed seven years of my life. A part of my heart and soul will never heal from what he did to me. But somehow, I just couldn't lie. I couldn't be that kind of person.

I knew Kobi would be humiliated and lose his job, and with two children to feed and at the age of 40, in Israel, it would be very difficult for him to survive.

I called Avi to explain that I was ready to tell the story, but it would only be the truth and I wouldn't talk about anything private or intimate. Avi said that wouldn't 'cut the cheese' so there was no deal, I wouldn't get my money. But he had another idea.

Avi had an older Brother who looked for company when he came to town. He said he was ready to pay - I wasn't stupid, I knew exactly what that meant.

But I thought, "It's just one night with this guy. Nobody has to know and I am fucking out of here forever."

I convinced myself, "I can do this. I'm not standing on the street selling my body. Many women offer this kind of service. They even pay for their medical school this way."

I decided that as it's my body, I could choose how to use it. I'd given it to so many others for free anyway, I might as well shift the balance, right?

So I agreed.

The man began calling me, making arrangements to visit my apartment, making it clear how he wanted it, how he wanted me. I hated his voice but the deal was the deal, one time, and I am out!

He told me that I'd need to wear knee length black boots, a black thong and nothing else. He wanted me to wait for him like that, so I did. The whole time I was shaking like a leaf. He rang the doorbell perfectly on time. I opened the door, dressed exactly as he wished. He stared at me, and I felt like I was about to vomit from his horrible, heavy, expensive cologne. He smelt like he'd showered in it. To this day, I experience the same nausea when I smell that stuff in the street.

He had big, greedy, blue eyes and he looked at me like I was meat at the butcher's.

"Good girl, just as I wished!" he said.

He hurried in and started to place his hands on my body straight away. I said I needed some water, and asked if he's like some.

As we sat down, I was thinking about ways to delay what was inevitable. His breath was stifling, he was heavy and sweaty and that cologne, yuck! My nausea was getting worse.

He took my head, forced it down and shoved his dick into my mouth. "Let's start working, shall we?" and he started moaning as he was moving my head up and down with force.

As if I didn't already feel like vomiting! I played with the idea of biting it's little head off. What a prick. So cocky and arrogant because he had money and I didn't.

I couldn't take it anymore. Tears were running down my cheeks into his groin and I just thought, "What kind of monster treats a girl like this, seeing her cry and sob, just to satisfy himself?"

I pulled myself away from him.

"I can't do this," I sobbed. " I just can't."

He told me that I was being stupid. He told me that many girls do it, that it's no big deal. He told me that he wouldn't be giving me anything and tried to force me to continue, shoving himself towards me again.

But I cried "I can't, I won't! Please leave! Now!"

So he got up, zipped up his pants and left.

I ran to the shower. I scrubbed myself again and again and again but his smell wouldn't go away. How could I ever forget how low I went? I decided I must never tell a soul. And I never did, until right here, right now.

I don't remember how I managed to get the missing money I needed for my flight, but I did. I bought my ticket and packed my bags. I couldn't wait to leave this life and all these bad memories behind and never come back. I celebrated my last days in Israel, saying farewell to people, clubbing and drinking.

Two days before my flight to Milan, Barak, one of the guys I would hang out with in the gym, called me.

"We heard you're leaving the country, so we decided to throw a party in your honor."

"Wow, really? For me?"

I actually believed him. I was thrilled! What way to celebrate my last 48 hours in Israel, with a party! For me!

He gave me the address of a private villa and told me to come along alone. Strange. I felt suspicious but I was curious and I wanted to know what it was all about. So I called my best friend at the time, Anna, and asked her to stay at my place.

"This is the address they gave me. If I'm not back by 2am, come and look for me and be ready to call the Police."

Anna wanted to know if I was sure about going along.

"Yes. If they're trying to trick me into something, I will teach them a lesson. I am nobody's toy. I will show them where the fish pisses from." (Israeli proverb).

So I arrived at the villa.

I remember it was all very white. Light background music, a couple on a sofa, and Barak. Some drinks, a flat white living room table, with money on it.

"Hi, great you made it, good to see you!" Barak welcomed me, then he introduced his friend and his friend's girlfriend.

"They just came to share some drinks with us. We did all this for you."

If there's one thing I can't stand it's being lied to. Being manipulated into something I might not want to do. If Barak wanted sex, all he had to do was ask. There was no need to play games and invite me to a fancy villa.

But that was not what he was looking for. As I got myself a drink, I noticed that in the centre of the villa there was a huge bed. I turned around and the girl was gone. Barak and his friend were whispering between themselves.

So that was what they were planning. To party with me all night, to exchange me between them and who knows who else or what else they'd thought of.

"I will keep cool, and leave them with their dicks in their hands," I thought.

Barak called me. "Hey, we got a surprise for you. I spent 2500nis (500e) on this for you today, so don't disappoint me!"

He spread some white powder on the table. Crystal. I'd heard about it before. I had never taken drugs in my life. I'd tried to smoke a joint two or three times but I just ended up with a sore throat and I hated the smell.

So, the motherfuckers paired up together (and who knows who else was waiting for me) to drug me with Crystal, Sex Cocaine, and use me for their own pleasure. All that while lying to my face and telling me they'd arranged a party for me!

Okay.

I decided I'd use all their Crystal, so their money would be wasted, and still not do what they were expecting from me. So instead of making an excuse and going home, I decided I would leave them hanging with their lost money and hardons.

Barak rolled me a 100nis and showed me how it was done. I leaned on the table, with the 100nis ready. I closed my eyes.

"My mind is more powerful than any drug," I said to myself.

"Whatever I do now, this will not affect me."

I said it to myself as if I was giving an order to the military troup. I knew I could control my mind. I put the 100nis in my nose and I sniffed all they had on the table, finishing everything they'd bought for myself and for them!

They looked at me, astonished. I stood up. I felt my nose going completely numb, buzzing as if it was covered in ants.

I kept thinking "This is not affecting me."

I smiled at them and said, "Now, if you don't mind, I really do have a flight to catch," and walked to the door.

They were shocked. "Don't go, we have a whole night planned! We've spent so much money!"

I kept walking. I started feeling heavier as I reached the steps, but I kept telling myself that my mind is my strongest weapon.

Just beyond the corner, I met Anna. It was 2am and she had started to look for me. I fell into her arms. We walked to my apartment, although it was more than likely she walked and dragged me there, put me into my bed, and lay next to me.

"So what happened?" she asked.

"The motherfuckers were going to drug me and pass me between them for sex, so I used their drugs and still didn't give them what they expected. I left them with their dicks in their hands and their pockets empty!" I said, laughing.

My nose was buzzing so hard I thought it might fall off. I fell asleep, and woke up after fourteen hours.

I had just a few hours to prepare to leave for the airport.

Anna was by my side.

"I am proud of you - you didn't let them take advantage of you." she said. "But you must be careful...you were brave and lucky."

I smiled. I felt proud of myself. My desperate for love, tortured soul finally got even despite everything that had happened to me.

Writing this story now I realise how lucky I really was and how silly I was to do what I did.

But I am not going to judge myself now. I turned my back on all my mistakes, all the heartache, all the blood, smoke fear and tears. I turned my back on all the humiliation, suffering and loneliness I felt in Israel.

I boarded the El-Al aeroplane that took me from Tel Aviv to Milan, and I changed my life forever.

Goodbye, Israel. Goodbye, Israeli Mirav.

CLAIM YOUR FREE GIFT

GET EXCLUSIVE ACCESS TO THE 3 PART VIDEO MASTERCLASS - The Undefeatable Method™

Discover my 3 step process to help you achieve any goal and go from stuckness, self doubt, exhaustion, breakdown, an 'imaginary dream' to conquering a goal.

STEP 1 - Let's get dirty!

Find your point A - your starting point based on where you are now. Get clean, clear and free of obstacles.

STEP 2 - Let's get wild!

Create your point B - develop a clear vision based on what you want and get detailed about your goals.

STEP 3 - Plan of attack

Create your path from A to B with a customised plan and a backup plan. Learn how to ensure that you'll achieve your goal, stay accountable and insert the mini-steps that lead to success into your daily life.

TO CLAIM YOUR FREE GIFT EMAIL

mirav@peppercoaching.online

Chapter 09
HUMAN ANGELS

"Vanity of vanities, all is vanity"

(Ecclesiastes 1:2)

I couldn't wait to land.

I imagined Rafael waiting for me in the airport with a beautiful bouquet of flowers or just one symbolic red rose. After all I'd abandoned my entire life to be with him.

I planned the moment carefully. I'd studied Italian during my final month in Israel, breaking my teeth trying to pronounce the words Dantè invented (obviously with a lot of imagination ☺).

I wore my best clothes and my finest perfume. I had my makeup done professionally by a wedding makeup artist, as well as my hair. I was 100% ready for this new chapter of my life. I wanted desperately to call this chapter 'Romeo and Juliet alla Mirav'.

Finally, after seven horrible years, I believed that it was my time to be happy. I wondered what Rafael's mother had prepared for me to eat. I visualised the look that would be on her face when she saw me.

I'd decided not to tell my own parents anything. I knew what they would say - I'm a man chaser, a stupid girl. That they're ashamed of me. That I should just go back to Israel. I couldn't bear this kind of discouragement.

My plan was to stay with Rafael in secret for a few days and then take the train from Brindisi to Milan, a journey of 16 hours. In Milan I'd work, make loads of money, cover all my debts back home and return to Brindisi to visit my parents feeling proud and rich.

Spoiler - life had completely different plans for me.

The plane landed. I collected my bags and headed to the arrivals hall. I was looking for flowers, anyone waiting there with flowers. But there was nobody waiting. My heart sank. I didn't know how I could use an Italian pay phone to call Rafael. I spoke very little Italian and my Israeli cell wasn't working here.

Suddenly, I saw him rushing into the airport. But his hands were empty. I was disappointed, but told myself he must have something special for me at home. Rafael looked nervous. He hugged me and held my hand. He was sweating and seemed anxious.

I felt like I'd taken all the trouble of getting my hair and makeup done for nothing. Rafael hardly looked at me. In fact, I felt like he was disappointed to see me! Maybe he didn't think I would actually make this crazy move and accept his invitation. Well, I was here now.

He took me home. His Mother greeted me with a warm hug and, of course, a huge lunch. She kissed my cheeks and had tears in her eyes as she looked at me. Rafael took my bags to his room, sat with us at the table for a little while, but then made an excuse and went out.

I was shocked.

I started to cry. I was tired from the flight, disappointed at his behaviour and missed Israel. I missed my best friends. I missed having my own space and my own apartment. I missed being able to communicate. But I had arrived and there was no turning back.

The next days felt so strange. I couldn't leave Rafael's apartment because I didn't want to bump into my parents. But Rafael was never around. I felt like he was avoiding me. His parents were kind and very sweet to me, but we couldn't communicate properly. Every time I asked them where Rafael was, they just told me that he was out.

The way I left for Milan was strange too. Rafael finally showed up and took me to the station. He hardly spoke to me, but as I boarded the train, he said, "Take care of yourself and call me whenever you need."

I felt relieved. He was there for me, so there must be an explanation for his weird behaviour.

So here I was, heading to work in a place I'd never seen in my life, all alone, not knowing more than five words in Italian. But I had no choice. I had to survive and I had to make money.

The train ride was horrific. I'd chosen the night train because it was the cheapest option. Every time I fell asleep I woke up to feel someone rubbing against my body. There were no guards and the train was small, crowded and smelly. I was scared to visit the bathroom and leave my bags behind.

I arrived in Milan at 7:30am. The group of Israelis I'd spoken to on the phone were waiting on the platform. They called my name and, for a second, I felt at home again. I rushed towards them. Milan was cold. It was December and I was wearing my thin, skin baring Israeli clothes. I was shaking, hungry and desperately needed to pee.

They took me to the hotel and settled me in.

"Aren't we supposed to have an apartment?" I asked.

"There were problems with that so we had to book this hotel."

I was sharing this room with a young man. A 23 year old with Brazilian origins.

The man who seemed to be the boss handed me a sandwich. "Eat, get settled and get ready to start work at 9am."

Shit. I was exhausted, the hotel room was tiny and I just wanted to go to sleep. But I got ready and went to work.

I was taken to one of the biggest shopping malls I'd ever seen and assigned to work at one of the carts. We were a team of five or six people. I was handed instructions written in Hebrew. It dictated sentences to say in Italian and gestures to make. I had to offer people in the mall a manicure, convincing them to try our kit and sell it to them.

Without knowing enough Italian, I was given a script to learn by heart. I hated it immediately, it felt so fake and a bit aggressive, plus I was never good at these things. I'd worked in call centers and customer service centers and I hated it. But it was a job. So I did it.

I worked all day long from 9am to 9pm on my feet trying to sell those ridiculous manicure kits. I managed to sell just one and I believe that only happened because the customer felt sorry for me.

I was starving. So at the end of the day I approached the boss. I asked to be paid daily as I was out of money and needed to eat.

He gave me 20 euros and I bought a sandwich and some water.

"You work on commission, but today is your first day so it's okay," he said.

I had no idea this was a commission only job. I went back to the hotel and tried to call Rafael. No answer. I called a few times but he never answered. The lonely cold feeling from years ago started creeping back.

What the fuck did I do?

I left my country, my home and my true friends for someone who didn't give a shit about me and a job that got worse by the minute. But by that time, I felt like I had no choice.

The next morning I dragged myself to work again. And again the next day I did the same. But I sold nothing. I'd spent my 20 Euros, and I had no food. I asked my boss for more money and he said he'd pay me later.

Back at the hotel, I started talking to the Brazilian about our lives. It was getting really late but I was lonely and fed up so talking to someone felt great. Before we knew it, it was 3am. Suddenly the door flew open. It was my boss. He seemed drunk and he started screaming.

"Do you really think I'll pay you for the shit job you're doing? I'm paying for your hotel and your training. I'm paying for you! You don't make money, you don't eat! I'll give you nothing. I'll throw you out of this hotel onto the streets and you'll be on your own!"

He stormed out of the room. He was furious and spitting fire. I was shaking. I couldn't deal with the violence. I had to get out of there.

I turned to the Brazilian. "You gotta help me!"

But he said he could not. He said he had a lot going on in his own life and that he needed to stay focused.

Rafael didn't answer his phone no matter how many times I called. I had no idea who to turn to - definitely not my parents!

I had that horrible, familiar feeling that there was nobody in the world to help me. There was nobody who would be there for me. That feeling can destroy you completely. The only thing that can save you is your own will to survive. Your determination to make life worth living.

Your dignity is all that keeps you from becoming desperate and, to be honest, your Ego. It's your Ego that won't let you lower your head, admit defeat or beg for help. It wants to prove them all wrong and show them that you can make it happen.

I will always be grateful to my ego for that. For protecting me from becoming a prostitute, dealing drugs, begging in the streets or worse. Most people talk negatively about the Ego, but that's because they don't understand it. It exists exactly for these situations when you have nothing else to save you.

Back in that desperate moment, I was trying to think about who the heck I knew in Italy, except Rafael's family (who didn't answer the phone), Anna (who now had a boyfriend and had disappeared into her own world) and my parents. I remembered a guy Rafael had introduced me to called Maurizio.

Maurizio spoke perfect English because he owned a youth hostel in Brindisi. Rafael took me there when we needed a translator. Maurizio was extremely friendly and had told me I could call him anytime. I think he knew long before I did that Rafael was flaky because he'd told me to call if I ever needed a place to stay.

I dug out his number and called him from the hotel to tell him what was going on.

I was crying so hard, I have no idea how he understood the words bursting out of my mouth while I was gasping for air between my sobs.

"Calm down. Listen to me. Go to the closest bus station. Get to the train station. Then take the train back here. Tell the control officers to give you a ticket, I will give them the money when you get here. You can stay in the hostel, we will work something out. Please don't worry about a thing. Just get here."

Finally, someone gave a shit.

I went down to the hotel reception and explained what was happening to the hotel manager. I don't think he fully understood but he did see that I was a young girl in distress. I asked him to help me locate the nearest bus station and so he drew me a small map, and wrote down the bus numbers and their times. It was 4:45pm and the bus left in fifteen minutes.

I was freezing cold with just a thin shirt on my body and Milan was snowing. The city was preparing for Christmas. I asked him to not say anything to anyone about where I'd gone and I ran to the bus station, dragging with me my heavy 22kg suitcase from Israel.. I got on the bus without a penny. I told the driver I was in trouble, but he shook his head and said nothing. I guess he saw girls like me every day, shaking in the cold, tears blinding their eyes, desperation in their voice.

He stopped at the train station and I dragged my bag behind me, feeling so weak and exhausted that I could barely manage to lift it.

A black guy appeared next to me, as if from nowhere.

"Let me help you." he said.

It didn't occur to me that he might actually want to help. I'd lost all trust in people, especially since my own people had betrayed me. Or at least that was the way I saw it.

"No thank you," I answered suspiciously.

But the guy came closer. He looked at me, and reached for my heavy case.

"It's okay," he said. His voice was kind and soft. He was an Angel.

I don't know if it was because I wanted so badly to be able to trust someone or because I was so tired, hungry and cold and my suitcase was heavy. But I suddenly had tears in my eyes.

"Thank you," I said.

He put the case down, looked at me again and asked if I was okay.

"Well, not exactly," I said. "I was tricked into coming here for work. And now I am here, with no money. I'm scared, I don't speak the language and I am running away from my boss."

He asked if I had somewhere to go. I was too tired to explain the whole situation so I said that my parents were in South Italy and I was going to make my way back to them. He put his hand in his pocket and handed me 50 Euros.

"Here - for the train, and something to eat."

I couldn't believe it. A complete stranger was willing to help me when my own people, my family and my so called boyfriend were not willing to lift a finger.

But I was proud so I refused. It didn't feel right to take money I hadn't earned.

"It's okay, I'll manage. But thank you so much," I said.

"Take it!" he insisted. "I need to go."

So I did. But I said, "Thank you, how can I repay you? Could you please give me your address or phone number?"

"No need, it's okay," he said. "Good luck!"

And he rushed away, disappearing into the crowd.

A ray of hope lightened my heart. It wasn't all bad.

I got myself a sandwich and boarded the train to Brindisi. It was a thirteen hour journey and I had nothing but my thoughts to entertain me. It was 7am by the time my phone started to ring because my boss had discovered that I'd run away. I opened up the phone, took out the SIM card, threw it in the bin and waited for the train to start moving.

It was a long, draining trip. The guard checked on me five times and each time I tried to explain the situation because I didn't have a ticket, but on the third occasion I was given a fine. I was lucky I wasn't just kicked out of the train in the middle of nowhere. Since I had no address for the fine's details, I gave my last known address as the one in Israel. I could now stay on the train for the rest of the ride without having to explain me being there every five minutes.

I was sitting next to a woman with a baby. We started to talk and I told her my story. She was about to get off the train, and handed me 20 Euros. Again I explained there was no need, I was going to find my parents and visit a friend and I would be okay. But she insisted and I took the money, wished her all the best and the train kept on moving. She was a second ray of light. Another angel.

I still had three hours' travel ahead when I decided this was a good time to pray. I wasn't religious, but after two completely unknown people helping me it looked like I was actually surviving this horror show. I felt I should be grateful to the one God I felt I knew. Besides, the journey was long and I had nothing to read. So I started reading the little Bible I'd carried with me for protection since my time in the military. My prayers had already saved my life once, so I decided that I might as well give it a try again.

As I read the poetic words, I felt as if they were speaking to me. They were encouraging me to keep on, to go on, to have faith that I would be okay. I thought about the two people who helped me and blessed them with all my heart, asking God to give them 70 times more than they'd given me, in every way.

"Shalom," a voice in front of me suddenly said.

I looked up from my Bible and a young guy was staring at me.

"Israeli?" I asked.

"Yes, Muslim."

Ah. We are supposed to be sworn enemies.

But that was in Israel. I wasn't in Kenzas anymore, was I?

The guy was my age. He was kind, gentle and well mannered. He meant no harm.

"Jamal," he smiled and gave me his hand to shake.

"Mirav," I replied and shook his hand.

The next few hours passed pleasantly and quickly. Jamal was from Haifa, a city near my own. He came to Italy to study medicine because he hadn't been accepted into medical school in Israel. He was going to Bari, a university city, just an hour and a half away from my destination.

I told him my story. We ate together and shared our lives happily. Our religious and cultural differences disappeared. Curiosity replaced them and we chatted happily in Hebrew.

"Tell me something," I asked him. "How is it to live in Italy? The truth?"

"The first two years are hell. No one will get you, you will feel lonely. It's hard to find a job and the mentality is different. But after two years, you'll be ruling your Queendom and using your mentality to do wonders," he said.

He was 100% right.

Jamal and I actually remained friends for another couple of years, until he finished university and returned to Israel. We visited each other, supported each other and hugged each other when we needed it.

He was always there when I needed him. I was also there for him. And he, together with the other two that day, were the proof I needed that there is light at the end of the tunnel. That strangers can sometimes be there for you more than your own people, that we should not let beliefs, religion and old mindsets limit us, and

– on top of all- that you must never judge a book by its cover.

I vowed that day to become the person who helps others in the same way I was helped, to never give up, and never lose faith.

Finally, I arrived in Brindisi. Maurizio waited for me at the station. He took me to the hostel and gave me a bed.

"You can use this one. Right now I don't have bookings for this room, and when there is a booking we can work something out."

I told him I'd stay a couple of days to recover my energy and decide what to do. He replied that he would help me out as a friend. He said that if he needed a hand in the hostel he would let me know and in the meantime I could stay and figure things out calmly.

My fourth Angel.

The next day I felt much better. I had something to eat, I took a shower and got ready for the day. And I decided to humble myself and visit my parents. I didn't want to take advantage of Maurizio's good heart and I didn't want to live with the daily fear that my parents would see me walking down the street.

I went over to their place and knocked on the door.

When they saw me standing there they looked shocked. But they invited me in, and I told them everything that had happened.

"What did you expect!" they said. "You come to a country not knowing the language, the culture, the people. You're chasing a guy who doesn't even care about you, then you go somewhere on the back of empty promises."

As if I didn't feel bad enough.

"We hope you're now ready to go back to Israel!" they said.

"I can't." I replied.

I'd burnt too many bridges there. I had no work waiting for me, only sorrow, bad memories and pain. I had loans to pay. Debts. And of course there was now someone else living in their apartment. That was something I didn't mention.

But, besides all that, I wasn't ready to go back. Not like this, like a dog with her tail between her legs. I wanted to go back with money to pay my debts and my fairy tale well lived.

NOT LIKE A LOSER.

My parents just laughed in my face. "Yeah, right. You will never get a job here. You are just wasting your time."

I told them I just needed a few months to see what I could do and asked if I could stay at their place.

"Our house, our rules," they said. "The only way you can stay here is if we book you a ticket back to Israel and that you stay away from your latest and greatest Rafael."

Again, conditioned. Again, rejected.

I just couldn't get it. Hadn't I been through enough? Couldn't they be there for me just once to listen to what I had to say, to support me despite my mistakes, the mythical "unconditional love" I was supposed to have as their daughter, instead of hurting me even more?

I have been through all kinds of prison lately. My freedom had now an unnegotiable value for me.

All I wanted was their love. Their approval. Their hug and some reassurance that it would all be okay.

So I refused their offer.

"I am sorry, but I am here now. And I want to try to make the most out of it. I am asking you to help me with a roof and food, that is all. I am not ready to go back to Israel."

"Well, then, you are on your own." They replied.

So, yet again, I was on my own. And this time I was on the streets of a country I hardly knew, with no language skills, no friends, no one.

So be it.

I went straight to Rafael's house. He wasn't there, so I tried to tell his mother what happened. She hardly understood and told me Rafael was going through some personal difficulties (years later, I found out those "personal difficulties" were another girlfriend he had at the same time I was around).

I decided to go back to the hostel.

Maurizio and I had dinner and I told him about what had happened. He calmed me down and said I could stay, for now, in the hostel. We would take things as they came.

We watched some TV and I went to my room. The cold loneliness, desperation, fear and the shameful feeling I'd made the biggest mistake of my life coming to Italy were pretty difficult to cope with.

I cried myself into an exhausted sleep, with no idea what my next step might be. I felt my parents' disappointment in me so deep in my soul, but I didn't blame them.

"I didn't think this through properly and I deserve to be punished for my stupidity," I thought.

But at the same time I was determined not to give up. I would, somehow, find a way to rise. To prove them wrong.

Chapter 10
ADAPTING

"To everything there is a season, and a time to every purpose under the heaven...A time to kill, and a time to heal; a time to break down, and a time to build up"

(Ecclesiastes 3:1,3)

With all that was going wrong, I still felt excited for a New Year.

Rafael fixed me up with a job. I was washing dishes in a cafe every day from 6am until midnight. I worked seven days a week for the sad amount of 400 Euros a month. Then I found another job cleaning toilets at a tennis club. I earned 5 Euros a day for that and I could do it whenever I wanted so I'd get up at 5am, clean the toilets at 5.30am and get to work at the cafe for 6am. I made 550 Euros a month so I figured that within one or two months I'd be able to buy a flight back to Israel without being a slave to my parents' rules.

I worked my ass off and hated every minute of it.

Italians in South are funny. I was considered stupid because I spoke such little Italian, even though I spoke three other languages, had three University degrees, spent two years in the Israeli military and had survived four wars.

They would mock me, make jokes at my expense and look at me like I was meat for sale (*note to reader; years later, when I spoke fluent Italian, I was treated with nothing but respect and admiration. It seemed that, for Southern Italians, it was important that even foreigners should speak their language).

I was ready to do almost anything to earn my keep. I offered to clean houses, to give massages, to teach private lessons. I understood my language barrier would either save me or break me, so I started listening carefully to the radio in the bar and people chatting.

It wasn't easy as they spoke in dialect, but with my focused attention and the shreds of newspaper I tried to read, I began to understand more and more.

I soon understood when I was mocked, and soon enough I was able to fight back.

In the morning, when I scrubbed the toilets, I would listen to Tony Robbins 'Live With Passion' and tell myself that it is all just a test of my resilience, a Cinderella story with a happy ending.

I worked myself to the bone, crying my loneliness out at night. But the weather and the stress started to become too much. I was eating scrapes and had no way to take care of myself. I started feeling weaker and weaker, and one day when I was cleaning the toilets, I fainted. A man from the tennis court found me, and called me an ambulance.

He spoke a bit of English and seemed worried about me. I explained that I had no medical insurance and that I was not registered in the Italian system, nor could I pay a private doctor.

On top of feeling weak, I had a burning feeling in my vagina, a burning that got worse by the minute. I didn't know how to explain it to the medics in the ambulance so I took a pen and paper and drew a fire. I pointed at my genitals. They took me to the hospital and I waited there for a doctor.

An old man walked in and looked at me with disgust. He asked for my documents and I gave him my passport. He put me in a room to examine me, together with three other young doctors, all looking at my bits, talking so much that I couldn't understand a thing.

He then told me to get dressed and said there is nothing he could do for me.

"I don't take care of women like you," he said.

I didn't get it. Later on I understood he believed I was a prostitute. I obviously wasn't local, I didn't speak Italian and I had 'fire' in my genitals.

I started to walk from the hospital to the hostel with no idea how

I'd actually get there, feeling worse and worse every minute, tears running down my cheeks.

A car stopped by me. It was Fabio, the guy from the tennis court who'd called the ambulance.

"What happened?" he asked.

I tried to explain.

He said he'd take me to a "real doctor" the following day.

When I went to work he waited for me by the tennis court.

He said he'd found me a doctor and took me to a house where we were greeted by a man.

"How are you today, Miss?" he asked in perfect English.

Oh thank God. I told him how I felt.

He checked me carefully, and said "My dear, it is just a urine infection which has become worse because it's not been taken care of. It could be caused by all the changes and stress you have been going through."

He gave me a box of medicine. I took the first pill and started feeling better almost immediately. He kindly walked me to the door and said that this visit was a gift, a way for him to show me that South Italy has also kindness. Not all doctors were ignorant and evil like the one in the hospital.

I went back to work and felt better by the minute. I was singing to myself as I washed the dishes and felt hope - not everything is always black in this world ☺ .

As washed the dishes, Rafael turned up for coffee. We chatted and he asked if I would like to go out with him the next day because it was New Year's Eve. I was thrilled! He had finally come to his senses - yuhuu! I couldn't wait! The cafe would be closed for two days and I would finally have some fun.

I spent that afternoon humming all the love songs I knew. I couldn't care less what people were saying about me, that they were mocking me and treating me like meat. All I cared about was that I was going to party with my Romeo. Finally!

By this time I was so busy with my happy thoughts that I didn't notice the guy who walked in. This was a guy who was about to become very important to me.

He looked at me and asked for an Amaro Montenegro - the city's famous 'digestive'; a liqueur locals would take to help them digest the five hour lunch and siesta they'd just enjoyed. It was delicious and very strong - I used my position in the bar to taste it as often as I could.

As there was nobody working in the bar- they were all on a smoke break, and it was simple to pour a shot of my favorite liqueur for this handsome man, I gladly did so and prepared a shot for me too.

After all, I was celebrating.

"Salutè!" I said and we drank our shots.

The guy looked at me. He had brown, magical eyes and I could feel he liked me.

"Sei una persona allegra," he said.

I knew it meant something about happiness. I shook my head.

"Ti piace ballare?"

I didn't know that word.

So I said I don't understand and signaled a question mark with my hand. The guy started dancing with himself and humming happily. I started laughing. He was laughing too and I said "Si.. ballare!"

"Domani? Balliamo? Io e te?" he asked, pointing at himself and me.

Of course. Now that I have a date with Rafael, the cutest guy is asking me out!

"No, domani no, I am sorry!" I answered.

He shrugged and said "La proxima volta" (Next time).

I had no idea what that meant but I assumed he gave up on me. Oh well.

He paid for his drink and went away, wishing me a good evening.

I finished my shift and went to the hostel, telling Maurizio tomorrow I would finally be out and with Rafael.

The next day, for the first time since I arrived in Italy, I did my hair.

I dressed in my best clothes and put on my makeup. I waited anxiously all day for Rafael to call. Finally, he texted that he'd come and collect me at 22:00. Great!

At 21:45 I was waiting with Maurizio in the lobby.

At 22:30 I was still waiting.

Rafael never showed up.

I tried to call him from Maurizio's phone, but there was no answer.

At 23:00 I went to his house.

His parents looked at me, sad and confused, and told me that he'd already left. I was puzzled, I didn't understand what was happening. I went back to the hostel, crying my heart out.

Maurizio hugged me and said, "Mirav, he is an ass. He probably has another girl somewhere. He just uses you when it suits him and you jump to his orders. Enough is enough. It is New Year, make it one you will never forget. Make a decision to clean assholes from your life. Now, let's go out!"

I didn't feel like going anywhere, but I also didn't want to stay in the hostel on New Year's Eve and do nothing. Maurizio ordered some pizzas, and when they arrived we drove in his car to the beach, sat there, ate the pizzas and watched the fireworks.

"Make your decision," he reminded me.

I looked at the starry sky and thought to myself, "I've been silly to not see this coming, but it is time to send this guy to hell."

I opened my mouth and screamed into the open air "Fuck Rafael!"

"Yes that's the spirit!" Maurizio said, and opened two beer bottles together, giving me one.

"FUCK EVERYBODY!" I screamed from the top of my lungs "AHHHHHHHHHHHHHHHH!"

I just screamed. I screamed until I had no air left, till I felt I took it all out. "I am never going to let him disappoint me again," I told Maurizio, and myself, as I sat on the bench, ate my pizza, drank my beer and felt in control again.

Rafael called the next evening. I answered, told him he that he was a coward and an asshole (I'd asked Maurizio to teach me those words the day before) and I said that I never wanted to see him again.

I slammed the phone down and put my trainers on. It was a

holiday in Italy and I could finally dedicate some time for me and my body. I put my music on and went for my long walk. As I listened to my tunes, a sense of pride washed over me. Here I am in Italy, alone, with no chance to survive, but I am surviving. I am working. I am learning the language. I even made a friend. I will be okay.

A car stopped nearby. I ignored it - it must be one of the horny Italian guys looking at me like fresh meat for sale again. But the car drove near me, following me, then the window opened and a somehow familiar voice said "Wei, bella!"

I turned to look. It was the cute dancing guy from the bar.

"Hey," I answered.

He asked me if I wanted a lift, pointing to the seat next to him with his hand.

"No, I am exercising," I explained with my hands too.

He extended his hand through the window and said "Gianni."

"Mirav," I replied, and shook his hand.

He smiled, said something I couldn't understand, so I just nodded and 'Ciao'ed' him, as he drove away.

I kept walking, smiling to myself.

I've still got it ☺ who needs Rafael, with so many fish in the sea?

I enjoyed the last minutes of of my free day walking in nature, watching movies with Maurizio and finally, feeling strong again.

What a way to start a New Year in Italy. Against all odds, I made it.

Chapter 11
GIANNI

"Two are better than one"

(Ecclesiastes 4:9)

I returned to work on 7th January feeling well and determined to make the money I needed to get the heck out of Italy.

I didn't care anymore that me, Mrs Big Shot with 3 degrees, ex military, Muay Thai champion was on all fours scrubbing mens' toilets clean.

I listened to Tony Robbins, saw myself as a temporary Cinderella and thought about how humble life forced me to be. I found a nice gym at the corner of the street, and the Manager let me train there free in exchange for teaching some self-defense classes for him.

I was thrilled - though I had absolutely no idea how I would do it when I was working 21 hours a day and knew nobody in this town. But at least I got to train and, whenever I had a longer lunch break or an early evening, I went straight to the gym and hit the weights.

Rafael turned up at the cafe from time to time, always offering me a sad look but never talking much.

Gianni, however, turned up every single day after work to have his Amaro. He always put a smile on my face with his silly dance moves. He started passing by at closing time to offer me a ride back to the hostel, a ride I felt more and more happy to accept.

Gianni always smelled good, and when he laughed his eyes sparkled. But that wasn't what made me fall for him - an event that changed all my plans forever.

One day, on the ride home, he asked me again if I'd like to go out dancing. My Italian was getting better and I had my dictionary with me at all times. I said I would love to, and we set a date.

The next day Gianni picked me up from the cafe and we went to a nightclub. I felt very uncomfortable as all the songs were in Italian and I was 'the elephant in the room'. I wasn't Gianni's girlfriend, nor his friend, so I felt all alone, and did what I always did when felt this way in public - I drank.

As the alcohol surged through my veins, I felt more and more confident. I danced, sang, and flirted with Gianni. By the end of the evening he asked if I'd like to come with him to his friend's empty apartment. I knew exactly what that meant and agreed. After all, I had no reason to play hard to get. I wasn't planning to stay in Italy, nor to conquer Gianni's heart. All I wanted was to pass the time nicely until I could buy my plane ticket.

We went to his friend's apartment and had sex. It was drunken sex from my side and I didn't remember much of it. In the end he took me back to the hostel and I thought to myself "Great, that's done. Now I won't see him again, and that's okay."

But Gianni surprised me.

He started coming to the hostel every time I wasn't working in the bar. My working hours were now a bit easier since another staff member had arrived, so I got one day a week off.

I started looking forward for Gianni's visits.

Although I had my schedule and daily plan in Italy, I was still very lonely and still hadn't become used to the culture, weather or food. I had no friends, and couldn't afford to call my friends from Israel. I could only email them and so I did, for hours every night.

It frustrated me I couldn't express my most simple desire or request due to the language barrier. I got used to the dirty looks and comments I would get in the street, but even when I learned how to say "va fanculo" (fuck you) in Italian, it sounded very strange coming from my mouth.

The painful feelings of the betrayal I'd experienced from my parents' refusal to help me were constantly present, and I avoided talking to them. I called from time to time but I'd hang up the phone, just to hear their voices. Then I stopped doing that, not wanting them to realise how pathetic I was.

Italian food was completely different from Israeli food. Israelis eat loads of fresh salads, hummus, tabouli, pickles, pita bread, with "schnitzel" (fried, breaded chicken breast) and potato purè, my favourite.

Italians seemed to eat pasta of different kinds at every meal, pizzas, focaccias and pastries. In Israel the only family-gathered meal was on Friday evening, and it was the longest one and lasted around an hour and a half. In Italy, families would gather together every day for lunch and dinner, which would each last 3 hours and include five different dishes.

Since I didn't visit Rafael's house any longer, my lunch break was a simple sandwich from the bar and my dinner was pizza with Maurizio, but I still missed the Israeli food, the smells, the language, the people.

I also knew that the more I stayed away from Israel the bigger my student loan would grow and I knew I'd have difficulties paying it. So I reminded myself about this every time I didn't feel like working (which was quite a lot - can you blame me? ☺)

It was January, and the temperature was around 13 -15 degrees, while in Israel it was usually around 40 degrees. My clothes were thin, and I was shivering most of the time - even at night, covered with 3 of Maurizio's hostel blankets.

One evening, as Gianni had visited and we were chatting in my broken Italian, I started shivering. He held my hands, which were ice cold. He looked at me with a worried face. I said it would take time for me to get used to the weather.

The next day, Gianni brought a bag with him when he came to visit. In the bag was a pair of warm pyjamas and a fleece blanket.

I had tears in my eyes as I looked at the gifts.

That was my first warm night in Italy, and that was the first time in a long time I felt my heart warming up as well.

Gianni started inviting me for occasional lunches at his house too.

Like most Southern men, he lived with his mother. At the time I didn't understand that his father was doing time in prison for homicide, which, of course, he claimed to be innocent of.

Gianni's mother had his soft, brown eyes, short hair, a beautiful smile, and she welcomed me into their home like a lost daughter from day one. I reverted to having an Italian lunch. It was a short version for me as I had to go back to work, but it was much better than the usual sandwich I'd eat sitting on a bench.

Gianni and I started seeing more and more of each other, and I started having feelings for him. I told myself to be careful, as I needed to stick to my plan to leave Italy as soon as I could, but the loneliness I felt without him was becoming stronger and stronger.

Then, one day, Rafael's mother called me crying. She said she missed me, that I needed to come to see her and that I couldn't just delete her from my life because Rafael was 'naughty'.

I cancelled my lunch date with Gianni and went to see her. We had lunch together, hugged, chatted, and sat on the coach, relaxing with an Amaro. She was just nodding off to sleep when Rafael walked in.

He seemed surprised, but very pleased, to see me and he asked if we could talk in his room.

I agreed, and with another shot of Amaro I followed him there.

There was no talking. Rafael just started having sex with me, pressing all the right buttons and ignoring my fading 'no'.

Well, I wasn't in a serious relationship or anything, and anyway I told myself that I was leaving this shithole. I left Rafael napping and went back to work, where Gianni came looking for me.

I wasn't ready to lie to him. I told him immediately I needed to talk to him. I told him I'd had sex with Rafael just an hourbefore. I said that it just happened, and explained I wanted to know how it felt to be with him (Rafael) again. And anyway, Gianni had never mentioned we were exclusive.

Gianni frowned and was completely silent for a while.

I waited patiently, understanding how he might feel. He then said that he would normally leave a girl after such a thing, but since I was honest, he would make a deal with me. He would let it go this time. But it must never happen again.

I was relieved and happy. I didn't want to lie, nor did I want to lose Gianni's company. But it was more than that. As soon as I realised that Gianni was jealous and wanted me all for himself, I felt pride. It was the first time since Kobi that someone wanted me like this and, as much as I tried to convince myself and others that I didn't need anyone, it felt good. I wasn't so alone any more.

I told Gianni I was planning to leave Italy soon, and that my deadline was approaching, along with my birthday in a couple of weeks. I didn't want him to fall in love with me just for me to leave and break his heart.

His answer was that we should just make the most of what we have right now, and think later about later.

Fine by me.

The days passed and the weather was improving as February

arrived. I finally had enough money to buy my ticket to return to Israel but first, it was my birthday. I'd always cared a lot about my birthday and found a way to celebrate, no matter what.

But this time it was different. I was in another country with hardly any friends or money to spend.

Gianni invited me out for a birthday dinner. I was excited and asked him if he knew where I could get my hair done. Getting my hair done for the first time in three months made me feel better about myself and my special day.

My heart pinched, though, every time I looked at my phone.

I'd just got an Italian SIM card and not many people had my number besides Maurizio, Rafael, Gianni, my boss at the cafe and my parents.

My birthday was my one sacred day, a day when everything should stop to celebrate my arrival in the World.

I prayed, from the bottom of my heart, that my parents would call to wish me a happy birthday.

My mother's birthday is actually two days before mine, so two days previously I'd decided to call her at home.

"Mom, it's Mirav. Happy birthday!" I said.

She just slammed down the phone.

I tried calling again, but nobody answered.

The pain in my heart was getting sharper and it increased with feelings of shame.

I was such a horrible daughter that my own parents kept turning their backs on me.

Not for a second did I think about how unfair it was that I was living at someone else's mercy, in a hostel just down the road from them, scrubbing toilets and washing dirty coffee cups for most of the day, while they are my legal guardians who brought me into this world, for better and for worse.

No.

All I thought was "I must be really shit to deserve all this."

A few months later, when I was beaten up, that thought came back and added "I told you so."

But, back to my birthday.

I held on to my phone all day long, watching messages popping up from Gianni and Rafael's Mother. They cheered me up but still, by 8pm I couldn't bear the waiting. I called my Mother.

She answered the phone and I blurted, before she could slam the phone down in my face again, "Mom! It is my birthday and you didn't even call to wish me happy birthday?"

"Well, what can I tell you? I am not fake. I can't lie. I couldn't wish you a happy birthday, when all I feel is disappointed in you. How could you do what you do? Living here in this country, cleaning dishes, running after men?"

Her voice became louder and louder, as the words penetrated my heart and tears ran down my cheeks ruining my birthday make-up and mood.

I put the phone down.

"What happened?" Gianni walked into the hostel lobby, seeing me in tears.

I told him and he shook his head and said "Tonight, we are celebrating your birthday. Adesso, non ci pensare!" (Now - don't think about it!)

"Gladly," I thought to myself.

We went to a restaurant. A handsome waiter started lavishing attention on us, surrounding us with wine and candles, bringing fresh bread, olive oil and salt to the table, together with 'Alioli' , 'Fave' (local sauces) and olives, which is typical at Italian restaurants.

I smiled at the waiter, checking Gianni for his response.

"This is my brother," he said.

I replied that I could see the similarity in his good looks.

"Ah! A glimmer of jealousy!" I thought with joy.

The meal was exquisite. Gianni and I drank and ate and laughed, I didn't want it to end, but I also couldn't wait to be alone with him in the car on the way home, where we would stop in the parking lot behind the football field and have sex.

A bald guy walked in and, smiling, approached our table.

Gianni hugged him, looked at me, smiled and said "Mirav, meet Danilo. My friend."

I shook his hand and he said "Tanti auguri!" (Happy birthday) to me, and sat down with us.

"Wow, Gianni has introduced me to his friend - that is a step forward in our relationship," I thought.

It was almost midnight and our meals were finished, when all of a sudden the lights went off in the restaurant, music started playing and the handsome waiter came to our table with a cake and candles.

They all sang at the top of their lungs "Tanti Auguri a te!" (Happy birthday to you)!

The cake was beautiful, with white cream on top and yellow writing "Auguri, Mirav!"

I blew out the candles, wiping the tears from my eyes.

Gianni and I had only been going out for a few weeks and I didn't expect this at all. He didn't seem like the man who'd be full of romantic gestures like this and this touched my heart to the core.

"You like the cake?" He asked "I asked my mother to make it for you."

My heart couldn't have melted more.

"I love it, thank you so much!"

We ate the cake and drank Limonchello, then drove away to the parking lot where we had sex. I went to sleep, almost happy, but not quite, because the bitter sting of my parents not calling me still lingered in my heart.

That evening I asked Gianni to take off the shirt he was wearing and give it to me as a birthday gift. I wanted to feel like I was sleeping with his arms and smell surrounding me. I slipped into his shirt, then into the warm pyjamas he gave me and went to sleep with the tastes and memories of the evening warming my bed.

I knew then it was too late. I had fallen in love and nothing else mattered.

Chapter 12
BROKEN

"Quod me Nutrit Me Destruit"

As Gianni and I became more steady as a couple, my plans to go back to Israel faded.

I didn't want to leave the one person in the world I felt cared about me, although Gianni said he understood if I want to go back to Israel and, although it would break his heart, he wanted me to be happy.

It wasn't his heart I was worried about, it was mine.

Gianni became my hero, my saviour.

From the day he brought me those warm clothes, took me out to eat, taught me some Italian and introduced me to his friends, I couldn't imagine my life without him. My days were lightened by his messages and visits, and the nights seemed endless and lonely without being with him.

I admired everything to do with him and about him, I loved how he dressed and smelled, I loved how he giggled, how he talked, how he made love. I even loved how he got, at times, a worried, angry look – which would never have anything to do with me.

Gianni shared his personal history with me. He was a father to 2 children, and his ex was 'dead to him' because she had cheated on him. He said he'd got so blinded by that fact he almost killed her.

He spoke about his father being innocent yet sitting in prison. He spoke about his job, which he hated, but paid the bills, his love of his mother and boats.

Gianni was a bad boy, and I was completely in love with him. His 'bad boyishness' only increased my admiration for him. I felt safe with him, I knew he would not let anything happen to me and that feeling was both new and addictive for me.

Gianni became my 'drug'. Even when I noticed the red flags

about him, I found a way to justify it. Gianni made the pain of rejection go numb and my loneliness finally took a break.

He was kind, protective, romantic, funny and took care of me.

Until one day, when everything changed.

We went to a bar to celebrate - I'd just got a job in an international school as an English speaking PI teacher. I was thrilled! No more scrubbing toilets, no more working 21 hours a day. I now had a 5 hour a day job, with lunch, paid vacation and a salary that would allow me to rent a room of my own instead of living in the hostel.

Gianni was happy for me, so we went to this new bar to have a drink. We'd just arrived when he saw someone he knew. He left me standing there and without a decent explanation or an apology he just headed over to talk to the other guy.

All he said was that I needed to wait there. He had that worried look on his face. So, I waited. Not knowing enough Italian meant that I couldn't even order a drink, I knew nobody and I felt awkward just standing there.

As the minutes passed, my awkwardness was replaced with rage. How dare he? I felt disrespected. He didn't introduce me to the guy, they were standing chatting and laughing, while here I was, his girlfriend, waiting for almost 20 minutes all alone, on a day when I was supposed to celebrate.

Gianni didn't even look at me to notice whether I needed anything.

That was enough. I waited 5 more minutes and then left the place.

I had no idea where to go to because nobody spoke English in this town, I had tears running down my cheeks and I just started walking aimlessly down the street, thinking to myself that an Israeli man would have never disrespected me like that.

A car stopped near by and opened the passenger side door.

"Get in." It was Gianni. I hesitated. But what could I do? Keep wondering in these unknown streets looking for the hostel?

I got in the car and turned to look at him, tears burning my eyes and I forgot even the few words I knew to express how I felt. I lifted my hand and slapped Gianni across his face.

I didn't expect him to react; in Israel a man reacting to that would be immediately arrested. I felt sure of myself and, I admit, a bit proud. Now then, he will learn his lesson. No one treats me that way.

Gianni looked at me, shocked. But before I knew what was happening, he lifted his hand and slapped me across the face with the back of it.

ONE. TWO. THREE. FOUR. FIVE. SIX. SEVEN. EIGHT.

I counted the slaps, feeling my back tooth loosening in my mouth and blood filling my cheeks.

I felt no pain, just shock, humiliation, shame. The burning on my cheeks was nothing compared to the tears burning holes in my eyes, everything moved in slow motion and I didn't even think of reacting.

I knew I deserved it.

It serves me right! I am in a foreign country, I shouldn't behave as if I was in Israel. I should have tried to explain how I felt, instead of using violence. Gianni wasn't a sucker. In my eyes, at that moment, he earned my admiration and respect.

Today, years later, I know why that happened. I know exactly what I saw in him in that moment.

I saw my father, punishing me for not respecting my mother, telling me I wasn't a good daughter and I deserved to be punished. I admired my father - he was a God to me. What he said meant a lot.

Here was Gianni, doing exactly the same. Punishing me. Showing me who's boss. Teaching me to respect him.

I didn't think he was wrong. I didn't think any of this was wrong. All I felt was shame. I told myself I could have avoided it, I made him do it, I deserved to be punished.

The few crumbs of self love that I had left were gone.

Gianni took me to the hostel. I hurried inside, hoping Maurizio wouldn't notice my swollen cheeks and the blood coming from my teeth. I went straight to bed. I cried into my pillow, put Gianni's shirt on and fell asleep.

The next morning was a Saturday. I went for my walk and Maurizio was out with his dogs so he didn't see my face. As I walked I tried to feel strong physically but on the inside I was broken. Gianni stopped by me in his car.

"I am sorry you are suffering, but you shouldn't have hit me. It could have been much worse, like I did to my children's mother."

All I knew in that moment was that I couldn't live without him. I couldn't bear the loneliness, the rejection or the cold any more. He was all I had. So I agreed and apologised. I promised I would never raise my hand to him again.

And I never did.

Gianni, however, continued hitting me.

In the next year we were together, he hit me four times and

each time there was a 'reason'. One of these times, he smashed my head against a wall because I tried to give him a goodbye kiss near his friends, and he didn't want me to. His Mother was watching and when he finished hitting me, she came to me and held my shoulders.

She was hit severely and often by Gianni's father when he was home, forced to wear unattractive clothes and have a short hair cut, wearing no makeup, according to his orders. But she loved him and her sons with all her heart, and couldn't make it by herself in this Southern city ruled by the Mafia and close minded people.

She had no money of her own and had been married since she was 16. She understood exactly what I was going through. So, as she held my shoulders, I was sure she would give me some of the love and support I needed so much in that moment.

But she simply shook her head and told me "You should have known better."

My fault, again. I insisted, when he said "No". I asked, when he didn't want to answer.

I was ashamed of myself, and looked at myself with disgust. In the year that passed, I'd become the worst version of me ever. The worst version of any woman, ever.

I had no character left, no dreams, no values, no dignity.

I was needy, pathetic, obsessive. I had no love for myself and at times even encouraged this punishment. It became so familiar that suffering even felt 'cleansing' to me.

I didn't care about anything but Gianni. I called him all the time, followed him, forced myself on him when he didn't want me to - no wonder he started caring less and less.

I didn't bother to ask myself what I was going through mentally. I didn't ask why I was becoming a shadow of a human being, I lost my appetite, couldn't sleep, couldn't function properly. I didn't dig deep, and no one cared enough about me to do so either. My parents wouldn't talk to me, my friends were far away. Gianni was slipping out of my obsessive grip.

The day he left me, I felt sure my world had ended. He'd got a job in Barcelona and explained that he wanted to be free and try out other girls. I couldn't stand the pain.

I went to his house at 5am to beg him, while he ate breakfast, not to leave me. Then I would beg his Mother to help and to talk to him. He had became my reason for living, and now I had none.

But Gianni insisted on leaving, and when he went to Barcelona I had to accept his decision. My heart was broken, but more than that - my soul was shattered. I had nothing left.

I didn't even know why I was alive any more. Part of me was too scared to end it all, the other part was hopeful something might change. Things might get better. And, the last part, was the Ego saving my ass again. Telling me to not give up, as everyone would expect me to. Telling me that I can't just die like this, with nothing to show for myself.

I was deeply depressed, but I had to keep working. My eyes were constantly red and swollen, my heart was in constant pain.

People who worked with me at school noticed, and started trying to help. Inviting me out, giving me advice, calling me. I forced myself to accept the invitations, so I wouldn't be home alone trying to call Gianni for the millionth time.

Slowly, I opened myself up to the new people who reached out to me. We started going out together. At first we were just two, then three, then we each time added someone new, until a few months later we had a 'gang' - a group of English speakers in

Italy who enjoyed each other's company.

But, more than that. My gang and my new friends found me funny, amusing, intelligent and a bit crazy.

Without Kobi, Rafael or Gianni in my life I had nothing to lose.

All my free time went to my friends and I enjoyed that more and more. I silenced my pain with parties, alcohol, and a lot of laughter. Soon enough a party wasn't fun without me. I tried to forget my broken heart in every possible way. I flirted, I went on dates, I had sex occasionally, but most of all, my new friends became my family.

I was always there for them, they were always there for me. For the first time in my life.

My confidence started to build again. With people around me who loved me, supported me, cared about me, I felt I was worth something again. I was still suffering because I only stopped hurting for Gianni a year later. I was still very confused about everything and I was scared to my bones of rejection. My fear led me to call my new friends 5 times a day, at times asking them for a confirmation they loved me, at times just checking they were still there. They understood and accepted this patiently. I just couldn't bear another loss.

My friends and their love for me started to heal my wounds. We all decided to start a diving course together, and although I hated having my head under water and my ears hurt like hell, I joined. We started diving every weekend and traveling for diving around Italy. I didn't love it, but I loved being part of our diving family. I wasn't alone anymore.

We went boat riding, diving, beach days, parties, and finally I felt better and better.

Then one day, I was fired from the school I was working in. I was devastated. I was blamed for something I didn't do, and was fired without questioning. I grieved the loss of my beloved work for two months, enough time to use the rest of my salary savings.

In the year that passed, I'd improved my Italian and built up some of my lost confidence. Also, after the break up from Gianni, I made up with my parents. They were now okay with me living with them for a while since my savings had dried up, probably realising that I was not going anywhere for some time.

I moved into their new apartment, relieved that I had a roof over my head and food I didn't have to worry about, yet I felt humiliated to have asked them to help me. I had to obey their rules as I was living in their house; that lack of freedom and the constant feeling I didn't truly belong there was a huge motivator for me.

I was never at home. I went out all day from morning until night, looking for jobs. The town didn't have any better work options for me. I couldn't go back to work in a bar or cleaning toilets. I spoke enough Italian to be able to work in gyms, but all 21 gyms in town only hired family members. I ran a self-defense course in the meantime, but the money was poor and people were flakey and didn't always show up for the class.

I talked through my options with my friends and one of them asked if I'd considered leaving Brindisi. There was a city near by which was considered 'The Florence of the South'. It's called Lecce. I had nothing to lose.

Armed with my new confidence and a bit of fake confidence I decided to do all I could to build the new version of me.

Chapter 13
REBIRTH

"And there was light"

(Genesis 1:2)

As if I needed any proof that the power of decision making is unlimited - Lecce was that!

Lecce was the place I also started to discover my true power. It was the place where I started falling in love with myself again. A place that healed me.

For years to come I would refer to Lecce as the place I was reborn in. A place which made me who I am today.

But, let's start with that first day. I will never forget it.

I got off the train at the station with a list of gyms I'd printed from the internet. Not having a car, nor knowing a soul in that city, I had to walk from place to place using maps I'd printed too.

Without foreseeing that, I was wearing my best clothes and my heels. Big mistake!

Eight gyms on my list, and I walked to each one of them, cursing constantly as sharp pains went through my heel-hating feet and blisters were growing all around them.

But every time I arrived at one of the gyms, I put on a big smile and ignored the pain, the sweat, the tiredness.

"Hi, I am Mirav. I would love to work here," I said with genuine enthusiasm.

When the Managers asked about my experience, I exaggerated and spoke about working in gyms in Tel Aviv, because I knew no one would know my city here and if I just said "Israel" they might not find that as interesting.

But Tel Aviv was famous in the world of fitness and everyone I spoke to nodded in approval and appreciation.

"What can you teach?"

"Everything you need," I lied again.

I was a weight room instructor. But all the gyms I went into had instructors already and I didn't think they would hire another one.

However I had absolutely no idea how to teach aerobic classes.

For the first time in my life, though, I felt I trust in myself to figure things out. I knew I had to do it, and I knew I could do it.

All eight gyms offered me a job!

I needed to give demo lessons on everything from Pilates, Yoga fit, spinning, fit-box, trampolines, spinning and whatever else.

I took myself and my sore, blistered feet back to Brindisi and spent the rest of the week studying all I could. I went through hours of different lessons, including ones about instructing and preparing steps to music.

Damn it, I had no ready music. What could I do?

I decided to bring in something original. I downloaded all the best hits I knew from Israel, downloaded a music mix program and started creating my own tracks.

By the end of the weekend,. I had my eight lessons prepared with eight different CDs.

I went to perform my demos, feeling as proud as I could be.

I had no experience. I had no connections. And, on top of it all, I still didn't know enough Italian. But I was determined to make this happen, and I had nothing to lose.

So I dove in, che sara sara.

I taught some of the best lessons ever. When I didn't know what to say in Italian, I said it in English or even in Hebrew or I just screamed!

People loved me. They loved the crazy Israeli girl with guts of steel and weird accent. They loved my music, my fire and my energy.

I lacked knowledge, skill and experience so I worked extra hard to satisfy my students. I worked with my imagination, my sense of humour and on top of all that, I worked with my love for the loyal, passionate and fascinated students who turned up time after time.

I worked fourteen hours a day, each hour giving my all. I loved every minute of it.

I soon obtained an Italian driving licence and bought myself a small car so I could travel from gym to gym easily. I spent all day working then returned to my parents house and worked on the next days' lessons and music. I was rarely unprepared.

I started making new friends.

People loved how I made them feel. They didn't realise that my fire was the result of my hunger and my desperation. They didn't realise I was fuelled by disappointment after disappointment because I was sick of living a life that was less than I desired.

All they saw in me was a contagious ball of energy and it was addictive. People came to my lessons feeling drained, powerless, weak and but left feeling unstoppable and on top of the world.

I started getting thank you letters, flowers and gifts. I was constantly invited to lunches, dinners and events. My self esteem started to rise.

I enjoyed my work and my clients more and more but feeling like I was still the girl who disappointed her parents, who ran away from Israel, chased men, humiliated herself time after time, and lied her way to work kept me living in shame. I still wasn't free within myself.

Until I met Dario.

Dario was a man who'd joined one of my Pilates lessons. On that occasion he was the only man. I'd used Shade as the background music that day.

At the end of the lesson he approached me and said "Your lesson was amazing, I really enjoyed it. But I wouldn't use Shade if I were you. It has sad vibes to it. People come here to feel uplifted."

I'd never heard about 'vibes' before that day and I was curious about what he said. So I asked him what had brought him to the lesson and he explained he'd been suffering with back pain.

I'd just completed a weekend of studying postural gymnastics in Rome and so I offered him a personal session.

He happily accepted and a few days later I treated him.

I applied all the methods I'd learned in Rome and gave him the best possible session I could.

When we were finished he asked me how much my fee would be. I replied that I didn't want to accept any payment from him because he was already a client of the gym.

Dario looked sadly at me and said, "That is the completely wrong approach. You will never be able to make money this way."

I didn't understand.

"When you don't ask to be paid, you offer a service and you don't request your value in return. Is that what you want to attract? Is this how you want to be all your life - working for other people in gyms and earning by the hour?"

I was shocked. Nobody had ever spoken to me about this kind of thing in this way before.

"I guess not," I said. "But I don't know what else I can do."

Dario smiled.

"You gave me a gift," he said. "I'm now going to multiply your gift and give you one too. Do you know what I do for a living?"

I shrugged.

"I'm a Life Coach."

I had no idea what he was talking about. I'd never heard of anything like it.

"I help people live their best life, conquer their dreams - what is stopping you from conquering yours?"

I needed a minute. What did this guy want from me? I had no money to give. He didn't seem interested in me sexually. What was he after? Why would he even help me?

I started crying.

Dario was quiet and let me cry.

He sat by my side and waited. When my tears faded, he said "Tell me your story. You have thirty minutes. Tell me all you want, then put it behind you."

I told him all that has happened to me as fast as I could.

Dario listened without expression. He didn't cut me off - he just listened.

When I finished he said "Okay. That was it. Now I want you to only look forward. I told you I'd give you a gift. This will change your life."

If only he knew how true that was.

Dario gave me a Life Coaching course, together with thirty other people. It was held for six Sundays, six hours at a time.

I showed up at the first meeting to a room full of people all eager to make their lives shine like never before.

Dario saw me and smiled widely "I am so happy you made it and decided to come."

I smiled back.

Dario started teaching, the room went quiet and it felt like magic filled the air.

I couldn't understand most of what he said. I brought my vocabulary with me but he spoke fast and, although I wrote down the words I knew as fast as possible, I couldn't catch up.

But my mind understood everything.

Without understanding what he said, I could feel my heart expanding. I felt warm tears running down my cheeks and when I looked up from my notebook, embarrassed, I saw everyone else was crying too.

Something in me shifted.

When I went home I'd look at my notes and try to figure out the gaps. I started buying all the books he recommended, in Italian, and sat down reading them with my vocabulary. It took me hours to read just one page, but the next week I'd understand much more of the magic in the room and it mattered to me.

We were given exercises to do at home that affected me deeply. I discovered self love like never before. I looked forward to each Sunday and when the course ended I was shattered.

Dario invited me to a meeting and I explained how bad I was feeling that the course had finished.

"You need to learn to fly solo, Mirav. I gave you guys very powerful tools but you must fly solo."

"But I am scared," I answered.

"Why are you scared? What is the worst thing that can happen to you?" he asked and continued "You will be mocked? Rejected? Thrown out of your house again? So what?"

"No," I said. "The worst thing is that I could be poor again, with no money to eat, or get in debt and go to jail."

Dario laughed.

"Well, here you won't go to jail for a few debts. Now, listen to me. What is your wildest dream, right now? How can you make it happen? Think about it. And go for it. I believe in you!"

I knew exactly what I wanted. I wanted to have my own gym, to be my own boss. But how could I start?

What would be the one, unique thing that I could do here that would give me an independent position and make money?

Aha! Krav Maga! The Israeli self defense system! I knew how to do it. Everyone kept asking me about it.

I was always asked by Italian Krav Maga instructors to come to their lessons and pretend I was testing their students.

I didn't teach it because I didn't know enough Italian and I'd forgotten a lot of it.

But Dario told me to reach for my dreams so I did.

I asked one of the guys in the gym to take a good picture of me and help me with the Italian I needed to create a simple poster that I could put up in the town.

Someone else helped me find a gym I could rent for a small fee.

"This Tigress from Israel is here to teach you to save your life!" it said, together with details of how to sign up.

Over thirty people showed up to my first course!

The other Krav Maga Instructors in Lecce were furious, but nothing could stop me now.

Although I suffered bad mouthing and criticism, I was determined to make this work.

Every time I made some money I'd book training with the best instructors in the world and kept improving my skills.

I was shameless, direct, sexy and almost rude!

Although I'd kept my work in the gym, I was eventually forced to make a decision between this work and my Krav Maga.

I chose the latter.

I taught crash courses, private lessons and annual courses all across the region.

Italy started to notice "The Tigress from Israel" and I was invited to teach seminars all over the country!

My prices were low because all I wanted was for people to know me and to cover my expenses and training.

Over the next six years I appeared in magazines, on stages and even on television. I travelled all over Italy to seminars and I enjoyed what I did to the max!

I developed a special, close relationship with all my students. I loved them like family and they loved me.

Teaching Krav Maga became the flavour of my life. I couldn't live without it. I had no problem teaching it twenty four hours a day, seven days a week.

I even invented new seminars that nobody had ever experienced before. I even invented one seminar done during a real flight in a private jet, seminars done at night, in night clubs, in cars, boats, shops... my imagination was endless.

I embraced fully who I was - a woman who had realised her power, her sexiness and her fierceness. A woman who wasn't afraid to be who she really was, even though so many people criticised and hated her. A woman who loved and was loved. A woman aligned with her purpose and was determined to shine, no matter what.

I had endless amounts of energy.

On top of my courses, seminars and personal training, I still taught in a few gyms. I dated, had a year long semi-serious relationship, travelled abroad to train, took care of myself and never forgot the skills Dario taught me.

Very quickly, it wasn't only Italy that noticed me. The whole Krav Maga world noticed who I was.

I received hate letters and threats to my life. But I got more letters of appreciation and thank you notes.

Then, one of the world's greatest Krav Maga organizations invited me to teach in Poland. I was so excited and thrilled that I couldn't wait to jump on the plane.

I didn't ask for any payment; I was satisfied by the fact that all my expenses would be covered and I could join the training camp they were hosting. It was a win:win.

Oh My God - little me? In Poland? Teaching over two hundred people at once!

When I got there, it was better than I could have imagined.

There were posters of me all over the place. There were even t-shirts with my face printed on them!

Men approached me handing over roses! It was a beautiful country with excellent food and there I was, living my dream teaching, training and exploring. I felt like I had climbed to the top of my mountain.

My trips to Poland continued on a regular basis. I was always excited to return and each time I'd go back to my Italian students with new ideas and inspiration.

But then, one trip changed my life, once again, forever.

Chapter 14
FATAL ENCOUNTER

"And another secret I'll confess to you
My soul went up in flames
They say that there is love in the world
What is love?"

(Bialik)

As I was preparing for my next trip to Poland, teaching in gyms and dedicating the rest of the time to myself, I had random relationships here and there and loads of flirts on social media platforms.

I was single, strong, sexy and I wasn't afraid to show it!

But one of these flirts was becoming more serious. After chatting on Facebook we started talking on Skype, and soon I couldn't wait for our evening talks.

His name was Arod and he was great with words, with flattery and big gestures. One day he asked for my address and sent me a gift box with chocolates, a funny card and a few other items.

I was surprised; men usually didn't pamper me like this, definitely not without even meeting me beforehand.

He seemed like the perfect guy. He loved pets, lived alone, was educated, good looking and had a great voice, which matters to me. He was a non-smoker, charming and self employed.

I once asked him whether he had a bad side because he seemed too good to be true. He responded he can 'give too much'.

I just thought to myself, "I'm looking for defects instead of blessing my good luck."

When I was invited to my next seminar in Poland, Arod said he would love to meet me there. He was also a Krav Maga lover and he was living in the UK.

I was delighted we could finally meet each other in person, yet I still planned to have my fun in Poland.

Poland welcomed me, as always, with open hands. I just loved every moment of it. The flowers, the beauty of it all, the food, the simplicity of the people, admiring looks from the men...they were all so big, so impressive!

I couldn't choose between them if I wanted to! I had plans with one of them, though, and we set time to be together on the first night I was there.

Arod came to the seminar on the second day. We met in the hotel and he was even better looking than on our Skype calls.

I was relieved and blessed my good luck.

We then agreed to go on a date together the next day. That night, I had some fun with my Polish date, enjoying - without knowing - that these were my last days as a single woman.

The seminar was going great and made me feel on top of the world. Arod was there, participating but watching me from the corner of his eye.

I was aware of him doing so and it increased the sexual tension between us. I never thought anything, apart from sex, would happen between us, nor did I want it to. I was completely enjoying being single and free.

The next evening we went out on our date. Arod took me to a highly acclaimed restaurant but when we arrived I refused to spend my time there.

It was all white, with no music, candles or wine glasses. There was no romantic atmosphere whatsoever. Arod was embarrassed and said this restaurant came very highly recommended by one of his close friends.

"It must be a girl who likes you and wants you all to herself, if she sends you on a first date with me to such a shit hole," I replied brutally.

By the look on his face, I knew I was right.

We left the restaurant and walked out into the street. I saw another restaurant just ahead of us which looked nice from the outside, and in fact when we had a look inside it was just as I wanted it to be; warm colors, soft music, candles set on the tables, wine glasses ready to be filled.

Without thinking further, I said I'd like to stay there.

It was a French restaurant. The meals were tiny and presented on big, white plates, the service was exquisite and the prices were sky high. I didn't care. He was able to afford it and I was certainly worth it, especially as I was planning to sleep with him by the end of the night.

"So, tit for tat!" I thought.

The meal was awkward. Arod didn't speak much except to make silly jokes about us 'eating little bambi' and I tried to fill in the silence with useless chit chat.

At a certain point, I got fed up of the atmosphere and turned to Arod to kiss him. He rejected my kiss and looked offended.

"You think you can just kiss me, just like that?"

I answered "Sure! Why not?"

Then he started saying he was upset I didn't like the previous restaurant as he'd put so much effort into finding it and I didn't even want to try it. Now instead we were eating tiny amount of food for top dollar.

EWUUU. Touchy guy! Seriously dude, all I wanted was a restaurant to set the mood so we could go and fuck (although I wasn't saying this). No need to get so soft about it!

"Fine, as you wish," I backed off.

Arod and I finished our meal in silence. He then paid and we ordered a taxi. He asked if I would like to stop 'for a minute' in his hotel, as he had a few surprises for me.

"Sure, cool" I answered.

Maybe he'd finally warm up to me. We went to his hotel. As we entered his room, I was surprised to see a whole table with gifts set up for me. An iphone, champagne, chocolate, a scarf, a t-shirt, a kubotan (self-defense weapon), with candles and flowers set around.

"Man, this guy is desperate. I would've fucked him for free!" I thought.

Arod prepared us some drinks and sat down. I asked for some music. I needed to drink to loosen up, as the atmosphere between us now was not only dense, but really strange. On one hand, he'd invited me to his room and had all these presents set up for me, but on the other hand he refused my kiss and didn't even try to do anything physical with me.

WTF was going on?

The music in the hotel was unfamiliar and Polish, so I asked to play on 'Poison' by Alice Cooper and I quickly drank 2 shots of Vodka.

Let's get the show on the road! I started singling and dancing, in what I thought was a sexy way, and Arod started smiling and giggling at my moves but still, there was no movement.

The song ended and I sat down facing him and asked him "So, tell me Arod, about you. About your life. Tell me something I don't know about you yet."

To my great surprise, he started talking about his childhood with tears running down his face.

I don't remember ever seeing a man cry before. And definitely not this early into a relationship.

He spoke about horrible things that had happened to him - total neglect from both his parents, being raised by his grandmother, being born with a silver spoon in his mouth but nothing else, never having his birthday celebrated, reaching out for drugs from kitchen tables as early as the age of five!

I was shocked, but I didn't want to hear it all. I didn't want to get attached so soon. I seriously only wanted to have fun.

When Arod stopped talking, I shut down my empathy and said "Well, Arod, it's about time you understood that you are an orphan. With the parents you have, it is better to consider them dead. Now stop crying and lets have sex."

He looked at me, shocked.

"No one has ever spoken like that to me," he said.

"Well, people live in fantasy-land most of the time. I know exactly how it feels to go through shit from your own family, and let me tell you, it's a waste of time to try to make things work out the way you want them to."

Arod still looked stunned, yet, in some way, relieved.

"All the women I dated before told me I should try to make up with my family, with my mother. Blood isn't water. You are the first to say this to me. This is so refreshing, it is a relief. Thank you."

"Yeah, no problems." I said.

He got up and hugged me, kissed me and took me to the bedroom. Finally.

The sex was okay but it was nothing as I wished it to be. There were no fireworks, multi orgasms or jumping off the furniture.

But we were both tired and I was drunk. I sat on the bed with him behind me, stroking my hair and kissing my neck.

"I could stay like this, for the rest of my life," he said.

"Wow, strange." I thought "The guy had just a standard sexual episode with me, and he is going all mushy. Whatever."

Now that we'd got the deed done, I took my gifts and ordered a taxi.

He gave me money for the taxi fare and said we'd meet tomorrow at the seminar.

Cool. I had 3 hours to rest before teaching.

I got back to the hotel and went straight to sleep.

The next morning, as I got up, I checked Facebook and Arod's page.

'Sauna. Pool. Training and Sex. Life is good here in Poland.'

WTF. Was he out of his mind? Writing things like that on his social media? This was freakin' private! You don't kiss and tell!

I was furious.

Tomas, the seminar manager, welcomed me for coffee.

"What's wrong?" he said "Didn't your date go well last night?"

"The date was fine, eventually," I answered.

"But look what he just wrote on his social media. The guy's gotta be a complete idiot!" I said, angrily.

Tomas agreed. "No gentleman would ever do such a thing. You should date only Polish men!"

We laughed and I went to teach the seminar.

Arod showed up and I avoided him the whole time.

At lunchtime, Arod came to talk to me.

"Why are you avoiding me?" he asked.

"How dare you write what you wrote on your wall?" I was almost shouting.

"Well, no one knows we were dating, what's the problem?"

I felt like smacking him straight in his face.

"It is social media! You don't kiss and tell! And besides, many people know we went out; one is the seminar's manager! You don't see me writing about that on my social media!"

"Well, to be honest, I had a reason," he said.

Yeah let's hear this, this has to be good.

"I wanted to make a girl jealous, as she seemed to be trying to make me jealous," he said.

I looked at him stunned.

"Are you fucking kidding me? You used me to make another girl jealous, and you are telling me about it! You are just plain stupid! Forget anything that has happened between us, I never want to see you again."

I walked away. As I got to my room, my phone wouldn't stop ringing.

"Please, I am sorry, I took the post off. I wasn't thinking."

He called again and again. Then at last he said he'd booked me a massage to earn my forgiveness.

"Well, I could use a good massage," I thought.

"Besides, if he went to all this trouble, I might as well enjoy it!"

I got to his hotel later on that night.

"Unfortunately, the massage was cancelled as I didn't confirm on time," he said. "But I am ready to give you one instead."

Fine, I was there already. Massage led to sex, a goodbye, and I went back to my hotel.

Arod flew back to England the next day. I didn't hear from him until I got back to Italy and saw some messages on my Skype account.

He wrote that he'd flown to the States for some unfinished business, but that he'd missed me and he wanted to talk.

I responded. "I am very busy with my training and seminars. If you really want to get to know me better, you need to come to Italy and stay with me. I can't get to know someone on a two hour date in a foreign country."

I was sure he would back off and stay put in England. But, instead, the next day he booked his flight to Italy.

Chapter 15
AND THEN THERE WERE TWO

"Whoso findeth a wife findeth a good thing"

(Proverbs 18:22)

Arod was supposed to be arriving in ten days. As much as I wanted him to come, I was also protective of my personal space and time. It felt like my life was about to be invaded.

I'd spent the last year living alone, partying when I wanted, dating or having sex with whoever I wanted, whenever I wanted. I ate what I wanted, didn't clean the house if I didn't feel like it, visited my parents, slept late, travelled. I was totally free.

Arod was going to come and live with me. My house was in a fairly isolated location and it seemed rude to leave him in a hotel since he'd booked a two week holiday to come and get to know me. After all, this would be the real test, or so I thought. If we could survive living together this soon then it had to be the real thing.

"Well, you can't have it all," I thought to myself. "If you want a serious relationship with a 'catch', you need to sacrifice something!"

In this case I was sacrificing my own space.

So for the next ten days, I went out as much as possible. Pubs, clubs, friends - I did whatever I could.

At the time, I had an old car and it kept breaking down.

On the ninth day before Arod's arrival I went out to a pub with my friend Manuela. As usual, we got tipsy and had loads of fun but the pub was in a valley where there was very little phone signal.

It was almost 2am by the time we left.

Unfortunately my car wouldn't start and so there we were, two very tipsy ladies, pushing an old car up the hill until we could find some help getting it started so that I could drive again. At the time it was hilarious. We couldn't stop laughing about how we were so drunk we'd managed to push a car up a hill and about how much fun we had together.

Manuela was a smart young woman, a Lawyer, and passionate about both Krav Maga and shooting. We had lots in common. But what really bonded us was the fact we'd both felt unaccepted by our families, that we both embraced our 'fuck-upness' happily and had decided not to give a shit about what the rest of the world might think.

I took Manuela home and I went back to mine.

As I walked in I noticed that my PC screen was lit up. I must have received messages or emails. It was almost 4am. My Skype was open and I saw thirteen messages from Arod. I only read the last few because they were long and I didn't scroll up very much, but what I did read turned my stomach in knots.

"You're just a bitch and a gold digger, like every other pathetic woman! I hope Karma does it's job and teaches you a lesson."

I was shocked. Why would he write anything like this to me, the night before he flew over?

Scrolling up I started to understand that he'd tried to contact me and when I didn't respond he decided that I must be out with another guy, that I was ignoring him and that I'd used him for his gifts.

Why give women gifts if your idea about them is so low? And what if I was out with another guy? I didn't owe him anything.

But, on top of all that, how dare he speak to me this way without even bothering to ask if I was okay?

RED ALERT.

After being hurt so deeply and so many times by men, I knew I should listen to alarm bells when they start to ring.

Something was wrong with this guy.

I started writing "Arod. Don't you dare come here tomorrow! I never want to hear from you or see you again." I started explaining why and what happened that night.

Arod responded immediately.

"I'm so sorry, I didn't know! I was so angry - this was the worst of me! From now on you'll only see my good side!"

He begged for another chance.

First the 'sex' post on Facebook. Now this. Seriously, this guy was too much.

"I don't care for your excuses. If you show up tomorrow, you'll have to take a flight back. I won't even come to meet you," I said.

But Arod became more and more obsessed. "I will come tomorrow, even if I have to stay in the airport on my own for days, to prove to you how much I care and that I'm sorry."

"Suit yourself," I responded coldly, and logged out for the night.

I knew, deep in my heart, that Arod had destroyed any respect I had for him.

He sent me messages endlessly. He flew to Italy and promptly lost all his luggage on his connecting flight. I felt sorry for him and went to the airport. I didn't bother dressing up or kissing him when he arrived.

I greeted him coldly with "You shouldn't have come here." And as we drove I told him that nothing would ever happen between us.

He had no money or clothes and he knew nobody. So I took him to my apartment so that he could go online and make a claim for his lost luggage. I made him some food and spent the rest of the day trying to show him how little I actually cared.

I don't know if I was just tired of him insisting that he wanted me or curious to see whether he could 'make it up to me'. Perhaps I wanted to give him a second chance.

In the two weeks he stayed with me he did everything in his power to show me how sorry he was. He cleaned every day, made us meals, filled the house with post-it notes telling me how great he thought I was, complimented me and helped me in every way he possibly could. He brought me coffee in bed and spoiled me like a Queen.

I must admit, I enjoyed it.

During those two weeks many of my friends met him and they were all deeply impressed.

"What a catch!" "Don't let this one escape!" they all said.

And I listened.

Arod was the best of all the men who came before him.

"What chances do I have to find anyone better?" I thought.

And he was completely in love with me.

I didn't see the fact that he had no phone and no family or friends contacting him as anything to worry about. I just thought that it was great that I had nobody to compete with for his attention.

I didn't see the fact that he'd left his life in the UK so quickly to be with me as strange. I thought of it all as proof of his love at first sight.

I didn't even think about the fact that he seemed to have no relationship with his parents. After all, who was I to talk?

I certainly didn't see the fact that he was trying way too hard to conquer me.

This was narcissism at its best.

All I saw was a man in love, and my great chunk of luck, finally!

There were only two flaws in my fantasy as I far as I could tell. One was that my heart didn't skip a beat every time I saw him. But I told myself that I wasn't sixteen anymore and that all the men who'd take over my heart before had always left me broken hearted.

The second factor was the sex. It was okay, but after years of experimentation with so many men I knew exactly what I liked. And Arod wasn't ready to go with the flow. He was cautious, traditional and boring.

When I spoke about my fantasies and what I wanted to happen in bed he looked at me like a hurt cocker spaniel, as if I was telling him that he wasn't a good enough lover. I tried to explain that we all have different tastes and preferences but the look in his eyes was enough to make me shut my mouth because I didn't want to hurt him.

"Well, I've had enough great sex in my life," I told myself. "This guy is perfect."

It's not like I didn't come. It's just that I missed and wanted the excitement and adrenaline that I'd felt before. But then again, nobody in the past had offered to leave their whole lives to come and live with me. So I decided that the sex was a superficial, insufficient reason to give up the idea of this relationship, I ignored what I was missing and I dived right into life with Arod.

Although I wasn't in love, I liked him and appreciated him

in many ways. I started to feel proud to be next to him when everyone was looking. I felt proud that I'd found this gem. I started to talk myself into loving him. It wasn't that difficult - he was charming and seemed to have learned from his initial mistake, and I was still so hungry for love.

After Gianni, I'd shut myself down, not allowing myself to open up to anyone. I was scared of being hurt again. Arod seemed like the last person who'd ever hurt me (boy, was I wrong!) so I let my guard down and let him sweep me off my feet.

After two weeks, Arod went back to the UK to get the rest of his things and start a life with me 'for good'.

As soon as he returned I introduced him to my parents. They loved him, which meant a lot to me because they had never approved of anyone else. Arod charmed them both, chatted endlessly and told them exciting stories about his travels around the world. Not only did he pass the 'parents test' but I even got a look from my father that said "Don't let this one escape."

"Don't play your usual shit with men, Mirav," he hissed. "This one is special."

I didn't feel quite so proud then that I'd caught this big fish with my hook. I only felt ashamed that my parents thought so little of me.

"They're probably right," I told myself. "He's out of my league."

Arod stayed at my place in Italy for the next few months. He didn't work and nobody expected him to because he didn't speak Italian. I, on the other hand, worked in eight different gyms every day. Arod did all the housework, researched my courses and taught some of my Krav Maga classes from time to time. But the numbers started dropping. My students wanted me to teach them, not him. I wasn't invited to seminars any more. Perhaps my 'strong single woman' charm had lost some of the shine once I had a man on my side.

Arod and I started teaching classes together but I hated it. He would talk too much and I had to translate all the time, instead of doing things my own way. I managed to get him some personal clients so that he could stay busy, but money was running short. I was the only one working and Arod, who'd said that he had savings and money in the bank after many years of work, acted surprised when he discovered that his bank accounts were actually empty.

I started to feel trapped and frustrated that he was in my apartment all day long, not working, not socialising and depending upon me completely. But I told myself that I needed to stick by his side if I was supposed to love him.

He'd tell stories about his experiences around the world with famous people, rich people and women. I started feeling inadequate next to him. How could I measure up to people like Kim Kardashian and Mariah Carey? Arod was a Bodyguard and knew how to behave in exclusive places.

My self esteem started to drop, especially when Arod started advising me, correcting me and helping me dress better, take better care of my skin and telling me to look in the mirror before I left home.

I was a woman juggling life. I didn't care much about what people thought I looked like, I was a hard worker, a good friend and a great teacher. I did fourteen hours physical work every day and had very little energy left. I believed that whoever liked me would like me as I am.

But Arod had lived for a long time in a plastic world where appearance was everything. I hated being 'fixed' by him but I knew he was trying to improve me so that I could live life to my full potential, which is how he explained it. So I allowed it to continue, while losing more and more parts of who I truly was.

He saw me as someone who needed to be rescued and who required advice and guidance. He felt that I should always be 'tip top' with shiny shoes and brushed hair. His Princess. It sounds familiar, right...?

For me, Arod was a safe place. He was the man who would take care of me, who wouldn't hurt me, who would protect me and who would love me until his last breath on Earth.

We both bought into a fantasy and we were both very, very wrong.

But, back to our story...

One Spring day, Arod and I were having lunch with my parents and spoke about the fact that we might have to spend the Summer in Ibiza because Arod had found work there and my salary wasn't enough to support us. My mother asked him whether he had permission to work in Europe, since he wasn't born in a European country. He responded that he had nothing but a UK student Visa.

My mother said that she'd thought that this was the case and that she'd asked at the city hall for some advice. There were two choices. Either Arod would have to be fully employed by an Italian, with a proper contract of employment and taxation status or he'd have to be married to an EU citizen.

I gulped. Was my mother pushing Arod to marry me? I quickly exchanged questioning looks with her, but Arod just turned towards me said "Right, let's do it! Why wait? I know you're the one anyway!"

I couldn't believe what he was saying. All my life I'd imagined getting married. I'd dreamed about a proposal. But I'd never imagined it would be like this. And as much as I was delighted, surprised and couldn't quite believe what was happening, I felt a twinge in my heart.

This was no reason to get married.

I told Arod I'd help him with all the paperwork, but I needed to know if he wanted to stay married or whether this was just a means to an end so that he'd have permission to work.

He looked me straight in the eye.

"I've never met anyone like you before," he said. "You are different from anyone else. I know you're the one for me. I have no reason to wait - I love you and I want to be with you for the rest of my life."

I kissed him happily and agreed.

We were engaged and decided to get married as soon as we returned from Ibiza. We'd only been together four months but we were living together and constantly together so we figured that we'd had 'ten times a normal dating couple' in time. We fought a lot but we figured it was 'passion and fire' and, on top of it all, my crazy, stubborn, over sensitive character!

We were poor but we agreed that it was beautiful we'd get to start from scratch together. And we had no idea what we were getting ourselves into.

Anyway, after a few weeks we left for Ibiza and spent the Summer there. My heart hurt as we drove away from a place which had felt like home to me after all these years - I'd worked hard to feel that way.

My friends and my Mother had tears in their eyes. The sight of my apartment, the city and then the country drifting away each step of the way tore me up. But I tuned to look at my Fiance, proud to be by his side and to be starting our lives together 'officially'.

I was ready to do everything it took to create a nuclear family of our own that would last forever and be completely different to his family and mine.

We sailed away from Italy into the new chapter of our lives excited and united together.

Chapter 16
IBIZA

"Favour is deceitful, and beauty is vain"

(Proverbs 31:30)

I hated every minute of it.

Ibiza welcomed me with hot wind and not so pleasant news - Arod and I had to live with another five bodyguards in a penthouse apartment.

He said he didn't know, but after all I'd endured over the previous years, living in rented rooms and hostels, being on the streets and relying on the favours of friends, I couldn't stand the fact that we had to share our relationship space with other people. Especially not as a freshly engaged couple.

Once we'd unloaded our things and dropped off Buji, my cat, we hit the closest supermarket for groceries. As we were shopping we heard screams outside and a police siren. I ran outside to see what was going on. A young couple had fallen off a motorbike. Blood was running down the girl's leg but she darted off with her bag held tightly in her arms, the police chasing behind her.

Arod explained that she was clearly afraid that the police would catch her with a bag of drugs. He'd seen this kind of thing before. I was shocked. Even though I taught people how to deal with violence and I'd studied aggression and mental illness, I'd never actually witnessed such a thing.

But that was just the beginning.

In the months ahead I saw things I could never even have imagined! People poisoned with drugs, sex in the streets, young girls almost completely naked walking down the streets, people who believed their money could buy anyone - sin city at its worst.

But worst of all, I saw a side of Arod I really didn't like. He changed from being someone who had no phone, being constantly there trying to please me and talking to nobody else to dived into his work as if I didn't exist.

I didn't know any Spanish, I had no friends and our internet wasn't working. I started looking for gyms so that I could offer my Krav Maga lessons. Arod would go to work for eighteen, twenty or even longer hours, while I was in the apartment with the other guys.

They all lived their own lives, rarely greeting me. I had to hear them having sex with random women, and I seemed to be constantly cleaning up the mess they left in the shower and the kitchen. I also knew they could hear me screaming at Arod how much I hated the place.

I tried going out by myself for coffee or a glass of wine, like I did in Italy, but it wasn't the same here. The Spanish locals weren't interested in talking to me, and the foreigners were either working or partying. I was a fish out of water. I didn't want to party, definitely not alone. I didn't take drugs and I was so lonely. The only place I felt okay was, as usual, the gym.

I wouldn't hear from Arod by phone or message all day. When he returned he threw his clothes down for me to wash, stayed on the phone to his clients and eventually fell asleep. When I looked for crumbs of attention from him he'd yell at me that I'd get him killed because he was so tired.

I tried, in every possible way, to explain to him how lost and out of control I felt. I just didn't understand this place and I missed Italy badly. But he was too tired to listen. He was earning money for us, he claimed, so I should just support him and stop complaining.

So, I tried. I tried hard. But even when I kept quiet, my anger grew and grew inside me. I snapped more, I became more aggressive. I expected him to satisfy my needs, physical and emotional, when he came back from work. I expected him to see how miserable I truly was.

Luckily, the Summer didn't last forever. Four months later, peace was restored. Arod's work was complete and we headed back to Italy.

We got married in a swift civil ceremony on a beautiful, rainy November day in Italy.

My brother came over from Israel and for the first time I saw him and my father in a suit. I was surprised and proud that they'd worn suits in my honour.

My best friend did my hair and her sister-in-law did my makeup. I was surrounded with love from the moment I woke up that day.

Arod didn't tell even one of his family or close friends that we were getting married. My male best friends drove him to the ceremony and helped him to get ready.

My mother organised the ceremony in the city hall and the reception afterwards. She was excited, helpful and generous in ways that I'd never seen before. I looked at my family with love and thought how wonderful it was that we were all finally united and happy on my special day.

My students from all the different gyms came along. Dario came too, hugged me tight, and whispered in my ear "I told you that you deserve to be loved. Enjoy this!"

We decorated the place ourselves the night before the wedding. We were up until 3am, prepared our own music and created a very low key event but I was still thrilled and happy to marry the man I believed would be my forever husband.

I knew we'd have to survive for the whole year on the money he'd made during the Summer so I didn't invest in a fancy dress or new shoes but I didn't care. I was in Italy, surrounded by my faithful students and best friends. I had the man I loved and who loved me right by my side. I was glowing. My wedding wasn't materialistic. It was about our love story, our 'Cinderella' story. At least that's what I told myself.

On our wedding night after the guests had all left, I waited for Arod to give me something - anything. I wanted a piece of jewellery, a special rose or a handwritten letter. My parents had made him a gift. I'd written him a letter and booked him a surprise spa day, but he did nothing for me. Bitter disappointment choked up my throat. I'd never got the proposal I wanted. I'd worn a cheap, poorly fitting dress and shoes to save money. He'd not called a single soul or told his family and friends. And now, there wasn't even a simple card for me.

The bartender asked me if I'd like a special drink because I was a bride. I smiled and asked for my favourite 'Porn Star' cocktail, times three! I drank my cocktails one after the other, reminding myself that this was my wedding, my happiest day ever, and I shouldn't have to think about anything else. Besides, alcohol promises good sex afterwards, right?

Wrong.

When we got back to the apartment I ran to the bathroom and vomited my brains out. Arod didn't offer me any help or ask me how I was. He was just angry that our night had ended this way as we collapsed into bed to have the traditional 'wedding night sex'. I snapped at him and said that he ought to be quiet, since he didn't even get me a gift.

We spend the next few days bickering, fighting and having anything but the honeymoon phase! We both wanted to believe that we hadn't just made the biggest mistake of our lives by getting married.

As we slipped back into our schedule, routine replaced the bickering. We tried with all we had to love each other and to give each other attention and support. I started work again teaching fitness and Krav Maga classes. Arod stayed at home, helping me in the gym from time to time and we lived off our Summer savings and my gym work. But money was running out and when Summer drew near, Arod decided that he'd have to go back to Ibiza to earn cash.

I couldn't stand the thought of him going there without me. I knew he would hardly call me and our newly-wed relationship would start to fade away. I didn't trust that Arod would stay faithful in a 'sin city' like Ibiza where women just throw themselves at every man and I didn't want to be lonely again. So I decided I'd go with him, but this time I insisted that we should live alone. Arod was busy so it was down to me to find an apartment for us. I liked the fact that he left these kinds of things to me and the fact that I was in control, so I totally missed the fact that making all the decisions had become a repetitive pattern.

All the preparation, the arrangements and the organising was down to me. There was no shared responsibility, no teamwork and we made no couple decisions. It was just me so if I made the wrong choice, it was all my fault. I just focused on being the best wife I could be.

This Summer, Ibiza wasn't kind to me. I managed to organise my Krav Maga training, which I looked forward to all week long, but the situation with Arod wasn't good. He devoted himself to work, pushed me aside, neglected my feelings and loneliness and ignored my desire for us to spend time together.

When winter arrived we stayed in Ibiza because travelling back and forth to Italy was too costly. Arod found temporary work here and there and I had my Krav Maga students as well as fitness tuition. But the gap between us was becoming wider. We fought a lot. Our fights became more and more violent. Arod met some friends through work and started going out with them, while I had nobody to go out with.

When I tried to talk to Arod and explain how I felt he called me wingey, naggy and obsessive. I became angry and would explode, at times, with violence. Arod didn't respond at first but over time he became more and more reactive and eventually our boundaries were almost completely erased.

We both regretted our behaviour and tried to make amends afterwards, but the cracks in the facade became deeper and deeper. I saw qualities in Arod that I didn't like at all. He seemed weak. He would speak differently or ignore me when he was with his friends from work. He would disappear without letting me know. He showed less and less empathy towards my feelings. I was lonely in Ibiza and I felt as if he used that against me, knowing that I had nobody else to support me.

I became more irritated, jealous and frustrated by the minute. I felt completely lost and my life felt out of control.

A year after our wedding, I became pregnant with Xai. We wanted a child and we both vowed to do everything we could to give her a good life. For the first few months of my pregnancy we worked on our relationship and on ourselves. It seemed like we'd finally put the hard part behind us and now it was time to be happy again as a couple and a family.

But when summer came and Arod was in 'work mode', he forgot his promises and forgot how much I needed him by my side. I swallowed that frog for the sake of my child. But our fights got worse and worse and as my belly got bigger I had less energy to fight back. The bitter taste of betrayal returned in my mouth. How could he go back on his words and his promises? How could he care so little while I carried his first child? How could he stay out all night, while I was alone in the apartment preparing the nursery for our little princess? How could he talk to me that way, when I was about to become a mother?

When he left for work I didn't know if I felt relief or anger.

On one hand I wanted him to stay with me but if he did, we couldn't stop fighting like crazy. I loved him and I loved our child but I had imagined my pregnancy would be different and the disappointments were piling up. Arod had never introduced me to his family, he'd never proposed in the way I had wished he would, he'd never got me a wedding gift and he never gave me the kind of attention I craved.

The sex never improved - it actually got worse and worse. I felt like I was compromising too much, but also felt like I'd had no choice. I'd married him and I loved him. We were about to become a family. I felt like I'd just have to live with the disappointment, the growing lack of respect and the constant gulp in my throat.

Arod went away to work, leaving me to deal with moving apartment, the impending birth, learning Spanish and attending all my medical checks alone. I knew he'd left to earn money but it didn't make it any easier for me. I was tired, drained and my family wasn't around me. I wanted to be strong for my child.

I didn't enjoy being pregnant. I felt heavy, tired and my back was sore. It felt like my guts were in my throat most of the time. I was lonely, with just a couple of good friends I'd made in Ibiza. I didn't have much to occupy me all day and my Krav Maga classes became emptier as I looked more and more pregnant. I imagined Arod rubbing my tired feet, massaging my back, caressing me lovingly and talking to my growing belly. Instead he was away working and he felt more and more distant every passing day.

I started to think about how I could change and become more attractive to him, to start healing my marriage. I ordered loads of self help books and started exploring what I wanted. I didn't speak about my needs and I was as loving and accepting as I could possibly be. This didn't help. It seemed like Arod felt like his behaviour towards me more was more and more justified. Indifference eciscalated to blunt offenses and insults. Cruel words became curses, pushes became shoves and the lack of respect became intentional insult.

I kept quiet as much as I could but this would often lead to an explosion, followed by a bitter fight. If Arod was away he wouldn't come home. If he was home, I'd walk out and try to cool off.

Chapter 17
MOTHERHOOD

"God can't be everywhere, so he created mothers"

(Ancient Jewish Proverb)

I chose Xai's name when I started Muay Thai at just seventeen years old.

'Sai' means 'forward' in Thai - a front punch is called a "Matrong Sai'. When I fell in love with Kobi and Muay Thai, I fell in love with the Thai language and culture that formed part of the training.

I loved the music, the smell of Thai oil and the words. I still proudly remember my fifty Thai words, all Muay Thai related.

When I heard the word 'Sai' for the first time I was stunned. It represented all that I wanted - the power to move forward, the first punch! The word landed softly on my lips and I promised myself that my first born child would have that name.

In Italian, 'sai' means 'you know'. In English a 'sigh' is a well deserved, relaxing breath and in Japanese, 'xai' was a traditional, lethal sword.

Arod, as usual, left the decision to me and I was happy that I didn't have to explain or argue. When I told him my choice he just insisted it should be spelt 'Xai' and not 'Sai'. As long as it was pronounced the same, I didn't mind.

I wrote a six page birth plan and had it translated into Spanish. I prepared a room for little Xai, knowing full well she probably would probably never use it because I wanted her with me all the time.

Xai was stubborn, even as an infant, and her due date passed unnoticed.

As I reached week forty three of my pregnancy, the doctors ordered an induction.

The night before the induction, Arod and I decided to celebrate our last night child free, and went to a restaurant. As usual, we started arguing in the car. Arod had lost all his limits and had no understanding that the stress he caused me was hurting both me and Xai.

He became more vicious with every word and when we arrived at the restaurant he refused to go in.

"Sit there and eat, take my credit card. I'll wait here. The last thing I want is to be seen with you."

Angry tears fell down my flushed face. The sense of rejection, disappointment and disbelief flooded through me. I tried to shout, cry, scream, beg and threaten Arod but he did not care. So I didn't go into the restaurant at all. I got back into the car and started to drive home.

All of a sudden, Arod grabbed the steering wheel from me and turned it in the opposite direction.

My heart sank - what the fuck was he doing? He was going to get us all killed! I slammed my foot on the break, looked at him in shock and jumped out of the car. I started walking. Arod, who didn't seem to care at all, drove away.

"I hope you die delivering Xai tomorrow!" he shouted from the window before disappearing with my car.

I walked on, crying, caressing my belly and talking softly to Xai. I promised her I'd always protect her. The hospital wasn't far away so I headed there because I'd felt some pain. I had no identification, no money and no way to get home and so I asked the receptionist to call Arod but he didn't answer the phone.

I ordered a taxi and asked the driver to wait downstairs while I went into to get some money for the fare. I got into bed and cried myself to sleep. My alarm was set for 6am and at 7am I'd have to leave to be induced. But at 5am I woke up with a sharp pain that felt like I was almost folding in two.

"Arod, wake up, it's time!"

Arod jumped up, grabbed the bags I'd prepared in advance and rushed us to the hospital. My contractions had begun so I didn't need the induction after all. Xai was on her way and so, without words, we put our weapons down. There didn't seem to be any place for fighting any more. This was more important than anything else.

I had a thirty six hour labour with unbearable pain. Painkillers didn't touch it. Arod stayed by my side for the duration, encouraging, cheering, loving me and holding my hand. But by the end of it I couldn't take the pain any longer. I was hungry, tired and exhausted. The doctor decided that Xai needed a forceps extraction. I'd learned all the Spanish words I needed but I was in terrible pain and couldn't remember anything. Arod hadn't bothered to learn any Spanish and so my frustration levels were extreme.

On October 29, 2015, at 15:15, Xai was born. Despite the incredible pain that took a long time to heal, my heart exploded as I held her on my chest and it became a hundred times bigger. I'd never felt anything like this before. I cried, laughed and kissed her beautiful little face that was still covered in my blood.

She was my own flesh and blood. I couldn't believe that she was there, that she'd come from me and that she was mine, my own creation! I couldn't get enough of her. All the love I'd ever felt in my life was nothing compared to this feeling.

The first few months of Xai's life brought peace to our nuclear family. Arod stayed off work and spent time at home with her. I finally had the space to heal myself. It took weeks for my bleeding to stop. I had recurrent fever and an infection so I had to stop breastfeeding.

I decided to study a Masters in Chinese Medicine when I was

four days postpartum but I couldn't sit through the lessons because I was in such pain from the stitches. I also couldn't wait to see my Krav Maga students. In fact, as a 'postpartum gift' I asked Arod if I could go to a training camp in Poland. He was happy to stay with Xai and I was happy to go, although I missed her terribly.

When Xai was three and a half months old it was my birthday, so we decided to go to the Canary Islands for a weekend of celebration. It was one of the most horrible vacations of my life.

The euphoria of having a new baby had faded and life had become routine. Arod and I started to insult each other again. I was healing slowly. But the frustration and anger I had towards him was choking me.

I still found myself having to take care of things for him all the time while looking after Xai. He had no interest in reading books, asking the doctors for advice or learning anything about parenting. Once again we were constantly fighting. On the night of my birthday he cursed me instead of wishing me a happy birthday. He refused to do anything nice for me.

Surprisingly, on our last night in the Canaries, Xai slept well and we had a few drinks in our room. I was still bleeding but Arod wanted to have sex. Finally! We'd hardly had any sex during my pregnancy and he seemed to want me less and less. Nevertheless, we had drunken sex and he came inside me.

"What are you doing? I didn't say you could do that!" I complained.

"Relax, you're still bleeding," he answered.

I was angry. We hadn't discussed the possibility of having more children and I wasn't ready for this. I'd trusted him to make that kind of decision with me but he acted as if it was no big deal.

Yet it was. Because that night I became pregnant with Gaia.

The pregnancy was hidden because I continued to bleed for weeks. But at the two month mark I noticed the strange, familiar feeling of exhaustion again and a slight nausea. So I took a pregnancy test in a public toilet and it turned out that I was seven weeks pregnant.

This time I was not as happy about it as I had been with Xai.

Arod had no work. I'd just given birth so I had no work either. Our relationship was at rock bottom. This was not an ideal situation for bringing another child into the World. I was worried sick. My heart could not bear the thought of an abortion, but I didn't want to bring Gaia into a world of violence, poverty and constant stress.

It was an emotional rollercoaster.

But when I told Arod the news, as usual he said that it was my decision to make.

The most important decision of mine and my child's life, and I had to make it alone with nobody to turn to for answers. How the heck am I going to make the right choice?

As Arod could stay home with Xai, I spent hours walking by the beach over the next few days, talking to my baby.

I went to see my doctor and told her how I felt. I told her that my marriage was rocky and I wasn't working. I explained that Arod was home all day and that I was scared to bring a baby into a world of chaos. She agreed with me and said that I'd have two weeks to decide to terminate the pregnancy. When she said those words I felt like vomiting.

I was never anti-abortion. I'm a strong believer that some people just shouldn't be parents and that in some cases, like rape, bringing a child into the world may not feel right (I'm not judging, just stating my opinion) but at the end of the day each person has the right to decide what happens to their body. It's their life.

But I'd never really had to think about this much, until now. The thought of my child's life being terminated felt horrible, even though she was no bigger than a plum.

My walks at the beach became longer and longer. I spoke to my belly all the time but felt like the fetus didn't connect with me at all. It was almost as if she wanted to be silent and decide for herself what to do.

When I returned home, I'd see Arod sitting on the sofa in his underwear and I'd feel rage rising.

Why isn't he doing anything? Why isn't he taking Xai out, doing something in the house or even freakin' trying to talk to me about this pregnancy? Is this the man I want to bring another child into the world with?

Am I doing the right thing, or just torturing a child for nothing?

The days passed by but there was no clear solution. I didn't have a single thought for myself. I didn't consider that I could become a single mother, that I might sacrifice my social life, my career and my body. I didn't think about the fact that I'd be tied to Arod with two children instead of just one. All I thought about was what was best for her and if she should be born.

On the very last day of the two week deadline my doctor had given me, I ran myself a nice bath and sat there, in the candle light, feeling the baby inside me. I didn't know if it was a boy or girl so I just caressed my bump and whispered in Hebrew.

"My beautiful baby. I don't know yet what the best thing for you will be. You know the situation I'm in. You make the decision about whether to come into this world. I'll take my supplements, exercise, eat well, visit the doctor, talk to you. I'll give you my all. But if you decide not to be born, even if I have to carry the pain with me for the rest of my life, I'll accept your decision."

I know. This sounds totally crazy. But it was the first time I felt a connection with my unborn child.

As I finished whispering with the words "I'll always love you," I felt a flicker in my belly. I wasn't sure if I'd imagined it because it felt so subtle. But it was enough - she heard me.

When I got out of the bath I went into the living room, sat next to Arod and asked if we could talk.

I said "We can't live like this. I'm pregnant and I take care of Xai. I can't work right now. You're not working and our relationship sucks. So here's the deal. If we want to have this child, you need to find a job straight away. You need a good, stable job, not three months' work in Ibiza and nine months sitting on your butt. We need to go to Therapy and we need to fix this. If not, I'll have an abortion. I'd rather do that than torture a child in this reality."

I didn't mean what I said about the abortion. I was trying to scare him into action.

When Xai was born he'd promised never to curse at me again, at least not near her. He'd promised an end to the violence. But his promises were empty, and in truth, so were my own. It felt as if our dislike for each other was too great to control.

Arod looked at me with disbelief and started to squeeze my wrist, bending it to the point of pain.

"How dare you talk to me like this? You want to kill my son!"

He was convinced we were going to have a boy.

I shook my wrist free and picked up Xai. It sounds selfish, but I knew he wouldn't touch me if I was holding her.

"I didn't say that. I'm saying that you're the man of the house. I've been pregnant for nine months and now I'm pregnant again. I have no work and no future here in Ibiza and we're stuck here all year so that you get three months' work and then we spend nine months fighting. We can't do this anymore. Be a fucking MAN!"

I started walking away from him with Xai in my arms but Arod was so insulted that he pushed me. He wasn't that forceful but I stumbled and hit my belly against the washing machine.

At that point, I freaked out.

"How dare you! I'm pregnant and you dare to touch me like this? You wife beater!"

The volume of my voice got higher and higher and Arod noticed Xai's little face, crumpled up with fear and sorrow.

"Don't shout near Xai. Look at her face!" he replied.

"Don't push me when I'm holding her! Don't push me, ever!" I answered.

I fled to the bedroom, packed a bag and stormed out of the apartment with Xai.

I called one of my only friends on the island. She was a police officer. Ironically she was responsible for domestic violence against women. She also lived alone and Arod didn't know her address. I spent the evening there, crying, telling her what had happened.

"I don't know how things will ever be okay for my baby," I sobbed.

We went to sleep but I woke at 4:30 in the morning to an

onslaught of messages on my phone. Of course it was Arod. The first one was a photograph of our apartment, with glass everywhere. Someone must have broken in and I immediately panicked - was he hurt?

But when I read his message, it was total Gibberish. He must have been hurt when he'd written it, or very drunk. I couldn't really understand it. He hadn't actually had a drink for a year so it didn't make any sense.

The next message wasn't clear either but I could make it out.

"Look what you made me do."

I was worried but Xai and my friend were both fast asleep and so I lay there until the morning when I called one of Arod's friends. I certainly didn't want to call Arod after the fight we'd had and these messages, but I still had to check if he was okay.

"Did you see Arod last night?" I asked.

"Yes and we got pretty drunk," he replied.

"Can you check he's okay?" I asked. I told him about the photo that I'd received at 4:30am.

"Sure," he replied. "He was pretty upset. He said you want to kill his son. I'm sure he's just crashed out now and everything's okay."

I called him again later that morning. I wanted to know if he'd checked on Arod.

"I went there, but nobody answered the door. I have to go to work, so I hope he's fine," the guy responded.

I didn't feel reassured. I was worried. I wasn't certain if something terrible had happened to Arod or if he was just ignoring everyone. So I decided to head over to the apartment. I wanted to get Xai's bottles and some clean clothes.

I waited until 3pm and made my way back home. I went inside holding Xai in my arms.

Arod was passed out, fully clothed, on the bed. But the sight of the apartment was horrible. There was glass and blood everywhere. There was puke and shit in the sink. The garbage bins were turned over and everything smelled sour.

I touched Arod's shoulder gently but he didn't move. I called his name and started to shake him.

"Arod, Arod. What's happened here? Should I call an ambulance?"

He opened one eye. Thank God he was okay.

But as soon as he looked at me he said coldly "What the fuck are you doing here, you fucking cunt? Get away!"

"Arod, this is my house too! And it's Xai's home. What a lovely way for her to see her father. How could you do this? How could you behave so irresponsibly, now that you're a father?"

He cursed and started muttering at me. He claimed I'd locked him out of the apartment and so he'd broken a window to get back in.

It made no sense.

"What are you blabbering about?" I said. "I was at my friend's house all night!"

"Just get the fuck out," he replied.

"No, Arod. Get up, get cleaned up and you get out!" I cried. "I need to clean this mess. I'm not wandering the streets or asking my friends if I can sleep over with Xai. I'm pregnant, and I'm the sober one here!"

I looked around me. The balcony window had been shattered. The whole house looked like an explosion had hit it. It reminded me of Israel. I felt my stomach rise into my throat - I couldn't stand this! Xai was crying in my arms and I couldn't put her down on the glass covered floor to play with her toys. Arod's hands were bleeding and his wedding ring was missing.

"Where's your wedding ring?" I asked him.

"Who cares? I don't know. I probably lost it when I broke in. How symbolic, ha? Now get the fuck out, cunt!"

I took a deep breath.

"Arod. If you curse me once more, if you don't get up and leave, I'll call the police."

He laughed.

"Call the fucking fire brigade! I don't give a fuck!"

"Fine." I replied.

Crying, I walked out into the hallway with Xai. I was shaking and I held her close. What should I do? If I called the Police, I knew it might make it worse. But the alternative was to let him lie there for days, trashing the house while I stayed away without food and clothes for the baby and missing out on the rest that I needed.

So I called the Police.

They came immediately and asked me if I was hurt. I replied that I was fine and that he hadn't touched me.

"Please," I begged. "Just scare him out of the apartment and I'll get it all cleaned up."

"We can't do that," the policeman replied. "We have to arrest him."

"No, please don't!" I cried.

But the officers looked at me with five month old Xai in my arms and tears running down my face. They saw the shattered glass and listened to the words of the neighbours who explained they'd seen Arod break into the apartment at 4am.

"This is not the right place for your child. He might get aggressive if he sees you," explained one of the police officers. He told me to leave while they arrested Arod. So I drove away as fast as I could. I couldn't bear the idea of Arod being arrested. I imagined how much he'd hate me for it all.

I drove back to my friend's place and explained what had gone on.

"Good," she said. "Maybe he'll finally learn his lesson."

"I don't want him to get a criminal record," I replied. "It's a stain on his character and will damage his chances of finding work. Plus, he'll never forgive me."

She explained that if that was how I felt I could go to the police and cancel my complaint.

So I did. Arod was free to leave after 48 hours. But not before he told everyone who wanted to hear that he'd gone out drinking to celebrate the end of his marriage to the biggest bitch in the world!

I felt so guilty. I'd never meant for him to get arrested. He would never forgive me.

As I write those words now I'm thinking "Pff...he deserved much that, and much worse!"

But at the time all I could focus on was this feeling that I'd disappointed him. I'd driven him to drink with my empty threats. I'd caused him to lose control and I'd humiliated him by getting him arrested. Now I'd lost him forever.

He turned up the next day to collect his things. I looked at him sadly and begged him to stay.

"I'm so sorry," I said. "I never meant for any of this to happen. I'll work on myself. I won't winge or demand anything. Let's go to a marriage counsellor and make this work. We have a child and we're about to have another one."

Arod said that he needed time to think and I promised him that he could have as much time as he needed.

In the meantime, I attended all my medical appointments alone. Arod didn't want to come with me. I promised I would not complain, and I'd found us a great family therapist and booked an initial session.

I kept my mouth shut, feeling that more and more of myself was being negated. But I told myself that this was all for the greater good.

We attended family therapy for a while. Arod spent the time blaming me for everything that had happened between us. I decided to accept the blame and move on. We were given homework, but I was the only one who did it. However, I stayed silent.

Arod came along to my fourteen week scan because the doctor was going to reveal our baby's sex. It was the only appointment he ever attended with me. Dr Gemma smiled as she checked the size of the baby.

She looked at me and said "I already know what you're having! Do you want to know?"

"Siiiii como no!" I answered, excited.

"Eres una altra nena!" She clapped her hands, smiling from ear to ear.

A girl! A sister for Xai! Two little girls. Oh my God!

Tears of joy flooded my eyes but as I turned to look at Arod, hoping to share this joyful moment with him, he stormed out of the room.

He was so disappointed that we weren't having a boy. He had been sure it was a boy. Everyone, including a psychic we'd visited, had told us that the baby would be a boy. How could they all be wrong?

"Who cares!" I said. "She's meant to be a girl. We can have a boy later on."

I would not let him ruin my joy.

But for the rest of the pregnancy, Arod grew more and more distant. He found a job a month later and was absent for weeks. I spent all day with Xai and growing my baby. It was just the two and a "half" of us. I started getting used to doing everything alone - the shopping, the cleaning and the medical visits. I found a babysitter to look after Xai and I continued to see the family therapist alone. I was determined to make this family work.

I'd tell the Therapist about everything that had happened each week and how I would shut up even when something really bothered me. I'd explain that Arod never asked how I was. He never touched my belly and he never touched me. I'd talk about how lonely and scared I was, but I kept up a brave, smiling facade. I'd often say how grateful I was that Arod was with me after all I'd done.

During our final session, the Therapist looked worried and

nodded.

"I don't know how much more you can compromise yourself, Mirav. How much more can you ignore what you really feel and what you really want? You can't just fix this yourself."

I drove home that day thinking, "Stupid Therapist! What does she know? Of course I can fix this myself. It's my fault, so I can fix it."

I never went to see her again. But, man! I really wanted to call her a year later to tell her how right she was!

When I reached the sixth month of my pregnancy I was looking for a name for my baby. I'd made a list of all the Greek, Egyptian and mythical Goddesses. I'd gone through The Bible, my family tree and the best suggestions on Google. There were endless ideas, but nothing felt right.

As usual Arod had no interest nor time because he was working full time off the island.

After weeks of feeling like my head would burst trying to find a name, I suddenly remembered what I'd done last time there had been a difficult decision to make. I decided that what had worked once might work again.

So I ran a bath, lit some candles and played some soft music. I sat there with the water running down my belly, caressing my bump and talking to my child with my eyes closed.

"My love, you've made it to your sixth month of this pregnancy! I'm so glad you decided to stay," I said.

"Now, please tell me what you'd like to be called."

I waited patiently, stroking my belly again and again.

A sweet sensation started to flow through my body and I listened to it. I know it sounds strange but if you've ever tuned into a message like this, you'll know what I mean. It has no voice or physical substance. It's simply a feeling.

"GIOIA." It sounded like 'happiness' in Italian, I felt. I repeated the word and wondered if I'd got it right. Something didn't feel like this was a one hundred percent fit. It was more like ninety nine percent correct.

"GIOIA?" I whispered.

"GIIIOOOOIIIIIIAAAAAAAAA!" The sweet feeling flushed through me.

I decided to take this experience with me and see where it led.

The next day I had coffee with a few of my friends on the island. Yafa, a French girl who lived nearby knew all my secrets. I told her that I'd decided to call my baby Goia. She had a strange expression on her face.

"What'?" I asked.

"Well," she said, "don't get me wrong, I like that name. But in France it's not a great word in slang. And you never know, you might want to live in France one day."

How true! I'd known that something hadn't quite clicked into place. So I hurried home, put Xai down for a nap and ran myself another bath.

As I sat there in the warm bathwater, I stroked my belly and asked the baby to be clearer about her name.

"Tell me, my love, what would you really like to be called? I know I was close, but this doesn't feel right."

The sweet sensation arrived quickly this time. It was sweet, but somehow it felt more decisive.

"GAIA," I felt.

I jumped out of the bath and turned on the internet. The Goddess of the Earth! Of course!

I looked at the numerology of this name combined with my own,

There were three possible ways to spell it - Gaya, Gaia and Gaea. Only one of these resulted in a numerology of eight.

Gaia.

I closed my eyes and touched my belly.

"If I've got it right this time, give me a sign."

To my absolute astonishment, the next few days were full of signs. I got a book from someone as a gift, and it contained an acknowledgement to the Goddess Gaia. I noticed that the restaurant under our apartment was named Gaia. Arod saw a yacht sailing on the ocean called Gaia and a friend of mine told me that he'd had a spiritual reading and received the 'Gaia' card. He didn't even know that I'd chosen Gaia's name at that point.

It could not have been clearer and it was always the same spelling.

The next few months were filled with emotion. It was almost time to meet Gaia. Although I couldn't wait for her birth, the gap between Arod and me grew deeper and deeper day by day. I felt scared and lonely. I took care of Xai all alone. I attended medical appointments, cleaned the house and planned my birth. Nobody was there to share this pregnancy with me.

The few friends I had in Ibiza lightened my day, but it wasn't enough for me. I was frustrated but I kept quiet because I didn't want to risk Arod saying he wouldn't be there at the birth. At that point I was hoping to convince him to stay with me forever. But

I felt ugly, undesirable, unwanted and unloved. All the tension, rejection and this feeling that I was living on 'borrowed time' was catching up with me.

I tried to fill my days by doing different things with Xai, but it wasn't enough to numb the pain of my failed marriage. I couldn't drink, I couldn't exercise and I couldn't complain. Arod returned from work once every three or four weeks. He'd throw his clothes down to be washed, spent some time with Xai but spent the least time possible with me.

I felt completely disconnected from myself and this feeling seemed to affect my unborn baby. The therapist was right. I'd been negating myself so much that I was shrinking and forgetting who I actually was. I'd forgotten what made me who I am. Right now, this makes me laugh. Me? The strong, undefeatable, 'take no prisoners' me? Who was this feeling defeated, disconnected, weak and lost?

Yes. It was ME.

My parents were still in Italy and we hardly had any contact. I barely saw the few friends I'd made in Ibiza. I couldn't teach my beloved Krav Maga or do anything I loved. I wasn't expressing myself. I lived in fear of losing Arod and having to raise my girls all alone. I was paralysed by that fear and the thought of giving birth alone. Today I know I could do it alone and do it even better!

Gaia was quiet in my belly. Actually, she remained quiet for the first couple of years of her life. It was as if she knew that I had no space, energy or capacity to give any more than I'd already given. The feeling of disconnection scared the shit out of me, even more than the idea of becoming a single mother.

What if I could never connect with her? What if I couldn't love her? What if Xai had already taken all the love I had in me? I couldn't imagine loving anyone as much as I loved Xai. How could I raise a child I didn't love? What kind of disgusting Mother was I to even think about such a thing?

I didn't dare disclose my thoughts to anyone. I just acted like everything was cool. But it was anything but that.

Chapter 18
EMANCIPATION

"There can be no rebirth without a dark night of the soul, a total annihilation of all that you believed in and thought that you were"

(Vilayat Inayat Khan)

As the months passed I started to insist on leaving Ibiza. I just couldn't see myself raising children in the place. It didn't feel safe and it definitely didn't feel like home.

Arod's boss had a branch in Monaco and so he suggested that I should check it out and look for a house there. So, seven months pregnant with Gaia and with a ten month old Xai, I did.

I decided to look around Sanremo, which is on the border of the French Riviera, because I spoke Italian and my love for Italy grew more and more the longer I spent away from the place. It was a steaming hot August and there I was, in the last trimester of my pregnancy, in a strange city where I knew nobody, viewing ten apartments every day.

I looked at thirty apartments but nothing seemed to be what I wanted.

I was exhausted. It was so hot and there were mosquitos everywhere. I was seven months pregnant and Xai was just starting to walk so keeping her occupied was impossible.

The Italy I remembered was completely different to this Italy. People here were cold, closed minded and rude, but I wanted to leave Ibiza and I wanted my family to be free, so I felt like I had little choice.

Day after day I visited agents, checked websites and walked around searching for the home of our dreams. Meanwhile, Gaia grew inside me, receiving less and less attention. My exhaustion was becoming extreme and patience was running thinner and thinner.

Arod, meanwhile, was visiting exotic places around the world alongside his boss, sipping from coconuts in Mexico or skiing in Switzerland. I felt more and more frustrated. I knew that he was doing his job and providing for us but it seemed so unfair that I was running around looking for houses, taking care of my toddler and going through this pregnancy all alone, when most of the time he didn't even ask how I was doing.

He didn't recognise the effort, the energy or time that I was putting into house hunting when I should have been relaxing and preparing for the birth. He constantly asked me to do things for him. I had to get these papers, make that appointment or send him more money. I was becoming really fed up. I felt like I was his secretary, cleaner, helper...anything but his wife.

On the rare occasions he came to visit he was either on his phone or fast asleep. When I tried calling him he'd ignore me. He constantly threatened to leave me in those weeks before Gaia was born and I was too scared to argue back.

A few days before I returned to Ibiza I finally found my dream house. It was perfect. It had five bedrooms, a terrace, a garden, a large kitchen and a jacuzzi. I could imagine the girls playing in the garden while we had morning coffee on the terrace. Maybe we'd even have a son.

The house was perfect so I asked Arod what he thought. As usual he said that he trusted me and that it was my decision. So I took the house. It was expensive, but with Arod's new job we could afford the rent and maybe even buy it one day.

I signed the contract, paid the deposit and flew back to Ibiza.

Arod came home a week before Gaia was due. He didn't bother to listen to my birth plan, prepare a hospital bag or interview babysitters for Xai ready for the big day.

I remember thinking that he didn't actually care about anything anymore.

On November 8th, 2016, I knew Gaia was on her way. I went to see Doctor Gemma and she laughed and dismissed me.

"My dear, you have at least ten more days!" she said.

She was wrong and I knew it.

As I was heading back home after a walk that afternoon, I could feel Gaia was ready to be born. I called Arod and told him to get ready. At 5pm my contractions started.

I contacted the babysitter, checked our hospital bags, took a shower and prepared a meal for Arod.

When he arrived home, I said "Go take a shower and eat your food. My contractions are fifteen minutes apart so we must go."

He complied, but my contractions became stronger and stronger and the pain became unbearable.

I was on all fours trying not to scream because Xai was nearby when the babysitter arrived. Arod had disengaged. He'd done nothing to help me. But I couldn't think about him any longer.

We got to the hospital at 9pm and Gaia was born naturally at 1:50am. I pulled her out of me, with the help of the doctors and a mirror! It was miraculous! She was so tiny, so sweet and so beautiful. But my heart was full of fear. I knew Arod was planning to leave me as soon as Gaia was born and I was afraid that the moment had come.

However he just smiled and stayed there with us. Forty eight hours later, we came home and Arod returned to work. So there I was. I had to raise a toddler and a newly born baby and heal from this pregnancy and birth with no help.

I asked me parents if they'd come to help me, but they told me that it was too far for them to come. I didn't buy that, either. So I engaged a babysitter for two hours each day and did the rest all by myself. Arod continued to work away and he hardly asked what I was doing. But his birthday was coming up and

I'd planned a lovely gift for him. I wanted us to have a night together so that we could patch things up.

I went on a mission to create a life changing experience for Arod's birthday. He'd told me once that he'd like to open up his spirituality, solve a few issues and work on his physique.

So I bought him a book that had previously made an impact on me. It was called 'The Monk Who Sold His Ferrari'. I booked him a spiritual session with an amazing teacher I'd visited a few times and I organised a Shamanic Reading.

I wrote him a personalised training and nutrition program and bought him a three month membership in the local gym. We'd be leaving Italy at the end of those three months.

I arranged babysitting for the whole night, booked us into a five star hotel and organised a table for us in a beautiful restaurant. I bought some sexy lingerie and waited for Arod to arrive.

It turned out that he was going to be a day late due to a delayed flight. So I rescheduled the whole lot.

But that night was one of the worst of my entire life.

As we sat there in the fancy restaurant I'd found, Arod was silent. He wouldn't talk about anything. I chatted nervously to fill the silence until I snapped and told him that this whole thing felt impossible.

We hadn't seen each other for four weeks and it felt like he had nothing to say. He just looked at me with an annoyed, bored look on his face and asked if I was going to eat my steak. Back then I wasn't vegetarian - that came later.

I responded angrily that I would not. I was trying to get his reaction but I was also feeling knots in my stomach. I was so upset and angry that he couldn't find a way to be nicer to me.

Arod took my plate and ate the contents. He did that for the following four courses too! When we left the restaurant, Arod was silent, but full. I was annoyed beyond my limits.

We drove to the hotel in silence.

Arod said that he needed to take a shower so I placed his gifts on the bed, which I'd covered in red rose petals. Then I undressed and put on these sexy 'nipple stickers' I'd bought from a sex shop in Ibiza together with my new sparkly underwear and a pair of heels.

Arod hadn't touched me for over five months.

He appeared from the shower, gave me a kiss and sat down on the bed to open his gifts but he seemed disappointed,

"I wanted to give you something meaningful," I explained. But Arod lived in a world where material things mattered the most and I clearly didn't get it.

I started to touch and kiss him. He played along to begin with and I happily decided that this meant that I'd finally get our marriage back on track. But then, he stopped. His lack of desire was obvious. A sharp, emotional pain surged through my body and I started to cry.

"Why don't you want me any more?" I asked.

Arod told me that it wasn't my fault but I was just too hurt to hear anything he said. I spent the rest of that night in tears and in the morning I rushed home to the girls. I was happy to see them but I knew, deep down, that my marriage was on the verge of ending.

Arod returned to work in Mexico. I recall telling him, on one of the rare times that we spoke, that I was tired and that it was difficult for me to take care of two little girls all day long by myself while I was preparing to leave for our new life in Italy, which was just a fortnight away.

Arod snapped at me. "You know, if you weren't such a jealous bitch you could've been here with the kids alongside me and everything would've been taken care of for you."

I felt angry. I couldn't believe that he could have taken us with him and yet he chose to go alone. He'd chosen to deny the girls this experience and rob me of a well deserved break.

The next thing I saw was that he'd uploaded a profile picture of himself to social media sipping from a coconut in Mexico. I couldn't believe his rudeness and this lack of empathy for me. I became even more angry, irritated and frustrated so a few days later when he called and asked me to transfer the rest of our money from our bank account over to him, it was easy for me to refuse.

Arod had taken plenty of money to Mexico and what was left was meant to cover our expenses at home, with a little left over in case of emergencies. I wasn't willing to risk it while I was alone constantly with my two little girls. Plus, it was a Sunday and the banks were shut and I was feeling sick.

Of course, the true reason was that I was FED UP. I was sick of the fact that Arod contacted me only when he wanted something. I was fed up of being secretary, driver, cleaner, cook and mother. I was fed up of being everything but a wife. I'd had enough of not being respected. I didn't want to be told that I was constantly spending 'his money' when I was just paying the rent and buying food and clothes for my girls. I'd had enough of being alone all the time, raising our two girls while he sipped from coconuts in Mexico.

So I said no.

Arod was furious. He told me that I wasn't a team player. He said that I wasn't a good wife - I was just a thief spending his money.

A few hours later an email arrived in my inbox.

"From now on, consider yourself a single mother. I can't be in a relationship where there's no team work."

I wasn't surprised but I was hurt and scared. And I felt guilty.

That was when I called Diego - the Shaman I mentioned at the start of this story - and ran to him in tears.

Arod never used the Shamanic Journey I'd booked for his birthday. So a few weeks earlier I'd used the session with the Shaman myself. Diego's ageless face and wise, 'old soul' eyes greeted me and I immediately felt protected, safe and unconditionally loved. I told him everything and he totally understood.

He always accepted and never judged. I saw things I'd never imagined I'd see during my sessions with him. But it was somehow more than that. I started understanding more and more, I started looking at life differently and I started to change.

Diego's insights were wise and transformational. Under his guidance I learned to take greater responsibility for my reactions to what was happening in my life. I stopped answering back to Arod's insults and I focused on what mattered. I listened more closely to my inner voice.

It was no surprise that I ran crying to Diego when Arod's email arrived.

"The bomb has exploded," he said calmly. "You've got nothing to be afraid of. Just choose not to suffer."

That felt strange to me. How could I choose not to suffer when this was so painful?

But I listened and learned and although this was one of the most painful moments of my life, it was the beginning of my true salvation.

Arod kept his word. He left the apartment. I asked him if there was anything I could do to save our marriage but he told me that it was over. I flew to our new place in Italy with Xai and Gaia, accompanied by a friend. I'd dreamed it was going to be our 'happy ever after' but it was not. Arod drove my car over to Italy a few days later with the final few bags. Then he left and we didn't see him for months.

As soon as the owners of our new home learned that I was a single mother, the dream became a nightmare. They did everything in their power to kick me out despite the fact I'd paid four months' rent in advance. They disconnected the gas, electricity and water. They slashed my car tyres, sprinkled salt all over the doorsteps, locked the gate and tried to break into the house several times,

I endured it all alone. Arod was not available and I was scared and lonely with no idea what to do. Diego's words about taking responsibility for everything kept ringing in my ears.

We moved to a new apartment and we were finally safe. I felt my love for and connection with the girls grow deeper each day and my fears about not being able to love them enough disappeared completely.

My will to make things work for my little family, to keep them feeling safe, happy, healthy and loved no matter what became stronger than anything I have ever known.

The power and knowledge I'd gained over the years, and especially when my marriage ended, was now priceless. It felt like it was worth all the pain I'd been through.

Finally it was time to focus on me.

Arod agreed to my request for a formal separation so I eventually found myself standing in court in front of him, our lawyer and a judge. I realised with huge sadness that my fantasy was over and my 'happy ever after' was shattered for good. We were strangers. But this realisation also brought a huge sense of relief with it. I experienced a profound feeling that it was finally 'done'.

I knew, in that exact moment, that I was also done with teaching self defense. I was done with violence, conflict and horror stories. I was done with fighting. I wanted peace. I wanted calm. I wanted harmony. I wanted joy. I wanted to focus on myself, motherhood and my Queendom.

I also knew that I wanted to teach everything that I'd learned through blood, sweat and tears. I wanted to give, to expand and to dare to become something I'd always admired - a Life Coach.

I wanted to continue to show people how to save their lives, just not in the gym! I wanted to feel that energy, that connection and the sense that I'd helped. I wanted to fulfil my soul's purpose.

That was when I met Jay.

When I found Jay, I was looking for a business coach. However he seemed to have a different style of coaching to anything I'd ever experienced before. He would dig deep into the patterns in my life that I hadn't previously noticed, he solved problems I didn't know how to solve and seemed to have an answer to issues that I wasn't even aware existed.

Jay was fascinated by my story. He showed me the turning point and the blessing in every chapter of my life and encouraged me to find out who I had become and what I wanted to do. I realised that I'd never given myself that time or that pleasure. It was the pleasure of actually getting to know myself!

I discovered that there is a ME beyond the excellent student, the good girl, the IDF Sergeant and the rebel. There is a ME beyond the poor, humiliated, abused, obsessive, needy girl. There is a ME beyond the loneliness, rejection and betrayal. There is a ME beyond the lack of love. There is a ME beyond what other people thought of me. There is a ME beyond the survival, beyond the flight and beyond the urge to run.

There is even a ME beyond motherhood.

I started the journey of identifying the raw, true ME and that journey led to, and accompanied, this book.

I fell in love with ME all over again. Or maybe it's actually happened for the very first time.

I am a code breaking soul and I was born to change history, to end the suffering of generations passed down through my family line, to introduce unconditional love to my children and to help, serve and empower others,

I was born to love, not to fight. But the fight within me has made me who I am, and for that, I will always be grateful.

Epilogue

Conquering the goal of writing this book has filled me with enormous pride.

My story will not die untold and my pain and suffering has not been in vain. Although I hope with all my heart that none of my readers are going through dark moments, if you are, I hope this book can help and inspire you to push through and never give up.

I've been through so much but I've also achieved much more. I've learned important lessons in my life, I'm a great teacher to my clients and mother to my children.

In these last few days I've conquered another big goal I'd set myself - I've moved my children to a city that I feel will be a better place for them to grow up in.

I've yet again had to face fear, change, decision making, loneliness and huge responsibility. It's proved to me how much I've learned and grown in my life, especially within the last year.

If I could give you just one piece of advice from my whole life story, it would be to never give up. Not on your dreams, not on your life, and definitely not on yourself.

Remember who you are, where you are going, and where you came from.

Remember it is you, and only you, who can live your life and make it great.

Remember that mistakes are part of our lives, not the end of them.

Learn to forgive yourself. Learn to love yourself - anyway.

And remember to set goals, to dream big, to live your life to the maximum and...

'Put some pepper into it!'

I would like to add how much I appreciate you for being part of my journey and putting this book on your lap to read. How much I feel you are part of me this way. Thank you so much for being here. For feeling for me, loving me and probably even hating me!

I am grateful to have you in my life and would love to get to know you better.

I'd love to hear what you thought about this book, what your favourite part of my story was and what lingers in your mind now you've read it.

I'd love you to share this with me.

You can find me on Facebook or email me:

mirav@peppercoaching.online

Lots of love,

Mirav xxx

About The Author
MIRAV TARKKA

Mirav is a Power Coach, Author, International Self Defence Expert and former IDF Operational Sergeant.

She's a woman on a mission to help courageous high flyers transmute their past and nurture their inner strength so that they can rise and create their best possible future.

Over the last 18 years, Mirav has had her fair share of breakdown moments. She had to rebuild her life from scratch so many times while dealing with a roller coaster of emotions – isolation, rejection, abandonment, feeling unloved – but she kept going, no matter what.

After a profound personal journey doing everything within her power to become the best, sassiest version of herself, she now lives the life of her dreams with her two daughters in beautiful Southern Italy. Mirav enjoys the kind of confidence, self love, self control and power in her life that she's never felt before. She runs her own business and rules her Queendom. And she takes no prisoners doing what she loves.

She's dedicated to helping others find their power, passion and purpose by tapping into their authenticity and unleashing their inner strength so that they can enjoy every aspect of life to their fullest potential.

Mirav believes it's time for us all to start living in technicolour, to feel the fire and taste the spice. That's why she created her Pepper Coaching brand and you'll often hear her saying that it's time to sprinkle some pepper into your life!

Printed in Great Britain
by Amazon

64267008R00129